World of TRAINS

Edited by Patrick B. Whitehouse

Picture Research Patricia E. Hornsey

HAMLYN/NEW ENGLISH LIBRARY

London·New York·Sydney·Toronto

Contents

Publisher's Note

Since this book was written a national co-ordinating policy has been formed for the preservation of British historic railway relics; this has led to the closing of the Clapham Museum and the collections being re-housed at *The National Railway Museum* in York.

First New English Library edition, February 1976.
Published by the Hamlyn Publishing Group Limited
London · New York · Sydney · Toronto
Astronaut House, Feltham, Middlesex, England
in association with New English Library,
Barnard's Inn, Holborn, London.
© Text and illustrations copyright New English
Library Ltd., 1973, 1974, 1976
Printed by Fratelli Spada, Ciampino, Rome.
ISBN 0 600 39345 3

Left: On the Denver & Rio Grande Western standard-gauge section with a Denver-Salida train in the Royal gorge in August 1966.
C J Gammell

GREAT TRAINS OF THE WORLD IN PICTURES

GREAT BRITAIN
Left: Britain's last Pullman train - The "Brighton Belle"
C J Gammell

GERMANY
Below: Working view from the Hohenzollernbruie, of Koln-Hbf in the shadow of Cologne Cathedral.
DB Film Archiv

AUSTRIA
Right: Driving trailer end of O B B Transalpin (Vienna-Zurich-Basle) electric push-pull train pictured near Klosterle in Austria.
Austrian State Railways

World of
TRAINS

General view of Euston station, looking south. *British Railways LMR*

CANADA

The Canadian National's Supercontinental threading through The Rockies near Jasper, Alberta. *CNR*

AUSTRALIA

Above: Commonwealth Railways GM Class Co-Co 1,750hp diesel-locomotive with Indian Pacific stainless-steel train. *J C Dunn*

Right: A Clyde-GM 1,750hp and stainless-steel train of the Commonwealth Railways at Nectar Brook, between Port Augusta and Port Pirie, South Australia. *M C G Schrader*

Below: The same train as above at Port Augusta, waiting to start to 1,051-mile through run to Kalgoorlie, Western Australia. *M C G Schrader*

FRANCE

Above: Ex-PLM compound Pacific 231K16 on the Fleche d'Or
at Boulogne Tintilleries in September 1968. *B Stephenson*

Below: French National Railways four-current express
locomotive Class CC40100 at head of TEE Etoile du Nord.
La Vie du Rail (Broncard)

11

JAPAN

Left: New Tokaido Line train makes one of its infrequent station stops. The NTL is Japan's only standard-gauge railway, linking Tokyo and Osaka, and it carries only express passenger trains formed of streamlined electric multiple-unit stock.
Picturepoint

SPAIN

Right: The Catalan Talgo headed by SNCF diesel-electric locomotive BB 67400, with the Alps as a backdrop. *'La Vie du Rail'*

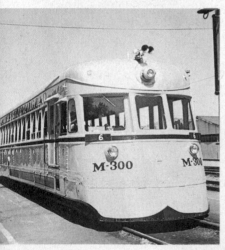

U.S.A.

Above: Diesel railcar M300 of the California Western RR pictured at Willits, California, in August 1969. *J K Hayward*

Right: New Haven line's Bay State New York-Boston train at New York 149th Street station in July 1961. *W E Zullig Jnr*

Top: Track maintenance in fairly common Canadian conditions, at Moncton & Sackville on the CN.
Canadian National Railways

Right: Tractor shovels are used extensively by Canadian National Railways for snow removal.
Canadian National Railways

BEHIND THE SCENES ON THE RAILWAYS

Railways against the snow

ON RAILWAYS in Britain Rule 78 of the Railway Clearing House rule book began 'In foggy weather or during falling snow', thus emphasising to all concerned the reduction in visibility during snowstorms and the corresponding increase in vigilance that becomes necessary. Everyone who has motored through a snowstorm knows the leopard skin pattern from the flakes which adds to the hypnotic effect of the swinging wipers and causes drowsiness and loss of attention, and that at a time when there is special need to see as far as possible through the murk and to beware of slippery surfaces. The difficulties of railway drivers in seeing through spectacle plates of steam locomotive cabs, which had no wipers, or peering over the side of the cab in the teeth of the wind and blizzard can be imagined. Such conditions account for a number of the more spectacular incidents in the history of railways.

As soon as it became accepted that the railway was a reliable means of everyday travel the need to ensure that it could work effectively, whatever the weather, became apparent and in the autumn of 1836 we hear of locomotives on the Newcastle & Carlisle Railway, which had opened in part the previous year, running with birch brooms tied in front of the leading wheels to sweep snow from the track as it fell. The wedge plough was introduced by 1840 and for that winter the Newcastle & Carlisle equipped all its engines with ploughs. It was not until well into the 1840s that it was considered necessary for locomotives to carry guard irons on the frames, whether bolted on or welded, to clear obstructions from the path of the leading wheels.

About the time when Charles Dickens was engaged in creating a jolly snow and stage-coach image of Christmas we seem to have had a succession of mild winters — which was just as well for the third-class railway passengers at least, for they suffered enough from the inclement weather when most railway companies thought they had done enough for them in providing open, often seatless, wagons, and trains that loitered interminably, either for superior-class trains to pass or for goods wagons to be added or detached. Only a few seem to have perished from exposure and the Gladstone Act of 1844 put an end to their worst miseries by insisting on closed carriages and 12mph from end to end of the line, all for a penny a mile. Many years were to elapse before enginemen could rely on an adequate cab to protect them from the rigours of the weather.

As railways expanded they traversed more and more exposed mountain ranges involving the crossing of wild moorland country and regularly began to experience the perils of deep drifts, expectedly in cuttings, but some-

times also in open country. The western side of Britain, because of the Gulf Stream, is less frequently disrupted by heavy snowfall than the east, and though the West Coast route crossed the 900ft summit of Shap Fell as early as 1846, the London & North Western line was seldom obstructed in the way that the North Eastern main line through Northumberland, at a much lower level, seems to have been. As a result the North Eastern Railway built plough vans that could be brought out quickly without the delay of fitting special equipment on locomotives, at the end of the 1880s. The first was built on the frame of a scrapped locomotive as a result of a prolonged fight against snow in the storms of March 1886.

A snow-clearing team left Gateshead on a Sunday night and forced their way up the East Coast line through a drift 1½ miles long and 14 feet deep, a feat which they probably would not have attempted in daylight. But they then came to a cutting where wet snow had consolidated into ice; they fought their way on from Monday morning until Saturday night without taking their clothes off. For 38 hours their only water was melted snow; food had run out, and when they got to Alnwick they had a celebration with several hams, roasts of beef and shoulders of mutton supplemented by three clothes baskets full of bread.

We owe that graphic account to Thomas Worsdell, the North Eastern locomotive superintendent; his new snowplough van functioned so well in improving conditions for crews that several were built. They gave great satisfaction in clearing drifts on the Durham moors round Consett and on the Barnard Castle or Kirkby Stephen line over the heights of Stainmore, with a 1,378ft summit. Coke trains from Durham to Cumberland and Haematite iron ore traffic in the opposite direction had been making big money for the railway since 1861 over the roof of the Pennines, but near where it runs alongside the Scotch Corner to Penrith road (known as A66 today) deep drifts were experienced; they have been up to 25ft deep of recent years, although since the Beeching regime the traffic now goes over the Newcastle and Carlisle route.

Worsdell was a chief who liked to see things for himself and so he accompanied a snowplough gang after the great blizzard of March 15, 1889, when the first part of the northbound Flying Scotsman became engulfed in snow at Longhirst Brocks north of Morpeth. Most of the passengers spent the night in the train, but to avoid having too many on their hands the Morpeth station staff sent the second part of the train back towards Newcastle, where it was thought the passengers could get shelter in hotels. Unfortunately what had been a difficult passage on the way to Morpeth had become impossible an hour or so later and the second part could make no further headway against the snow beyond

15

Annitsford, between Cramlington and Killingworth. Worsdell's snowplough party drew alongside them there and decided to return to a crossover at Killingworth and go northward on the up line, shifting the snow until the train was reached. The dangers of the move in darkness and driving snow, when the engine head lamps could hardly be seen a few yards away, were fully realised.

There were four ensuing behind the plough van and it was decided to use an overbridge as a marker where steam was to be shut off and the brakes applied. Whether one of the drivers failed to close his regulator or whether the ensuring collision was due to the snowplough unit sliding over the icy rails seems uncertain, but slide it did. Backed by the 300-ton mass of the four locomotives the wedge of the plough went under the leading engine of the train, which fell on the van and crushed it. Three of the men in the plough van escaped with a shaking from the matchwood remains, including a journalist who was out to see what Worsdell's new equipment could do. Unfortunately another friend of Worsdell's was crushed by the hot stove with fatal results and the locomotive superintendent himself received severe injuries from snatch blocks and jacks which were hurled to the front of the van. He did not fully recover and retired soon afterwards at the early age of 53.

When the Midland main line was completed up the western side of the Pennines from Settle to Carlisle in 1875, snow ploughs became a regular part of the winter scene. They were kept in readiness on pairs of 0-6-0 goods engines, coupled back to back with a tool van between them and able to clear the line working in either direction. Feats of endurance by the Carlisle and Hellifield plough teams in defeating the worst efforts of the snow fiend in the bleak Pennine uplands went into railway legend. West of the wild stretches of Langstrothdale Chase the railway takes advantage of Ribblesdale to climb for 15 miles, almost all at 1 in 100, skirting Ingleborough and Whernside before plunging into the depths of the 1½-mile Blea Moor tunnel, where in winter black icicles accumulated in the ventilation shafts. From a summit inside the tunnel there is an undulating road to Ais Gill, the 1,169ft peak of the whole line and then a 48-mile drop to Carlisle, beginning with several miles of 1 in 100 across Mallerstang Common.

Garsdale, the one-time Hawes Junction, is so exposed that the wind once caught a locomotive on the turntable and whirled it round and round like a teetotum. To avoid the need for enormous bogie tenders on the locomotives of through expresses, water troughs were put in just south of Garsdale, on one of the short stretches of level track, in 1907. They soon distinguished themselves by freezing solid and afterwards were steam-heated. They enabled an economical modernisation of the old snowplough arrangements by freeing four old bogie tenders to make the underframes of snowplough vans similar to those the North Eastern had had for three decades; they were introduced by whizzkid Superintendent Paget for the winter of 1909. With tools, cooking facilities and other comforts for the crews they could be attached to any engine available and the waste of engines standing by in steam for snowplough work all through the winter, in fine weather or foul, came to an end.

Sometimes the dangers of blizzards of wet snow in freezing temperatures, to which most of Britain is subject from time to time, were brought home to railwaymen in

lowland country, as at Abbots Ripton in 1876, this part of Huntingdonshire was swept by a heavy fall of snow accompanied by a north-easterly gale. At that time the Great Northern block system was based on normal clear and 'clear' was indicated by the semaphore arms dropping into slots in the posts and exhibition of a white light.

Tragedy built up slowly through the sluggish reactions of several of those concerned. A 37-wagon coal train lumbered south from Peterborough through the darkness and driving snow and was intended to shunt at Holme to get out of the path of the up Flying Scotsman. The crew saw only clear signals and went through Holme; the signalman there had no means of telegraphing to the next two boxes, Conington and Wood Walton, so he did the next best thing and sent a message to Abbots Ripton to shunt the coal train there. The Abbots Ripton signalman stopped it by waving a red lamp and the shunt into a siding began. The Scotsman meanwhile was following on and keeping good time despite the storm; the Holme stationmaster was afterwards censured for not having stopped it and warned that crew that a goods train had run through the Holme signals. The express crew also saw only clear signals and collided with the last six coal wagons and the engine, still on the main line. Debris was scattered over both tracks.

The Abbots Ripton men set out to protect the line, and in addition the coal engine went forward to warn an expected northbound express. Unhappily the signalman did not send obstruction danger on his block instrument to the next box, Stukeley, but wasted time trying to get a telegraph message through to Huntingdon to intercept the down train there. When he rang Stukeley it was too late. Although the down express had passed that box the warnings from the lineside and from the coal engine might have been effective but for the paucity of brake power. So the Leeds express, which had run into the storm at St Neots and with the driver peering over the side of his cab into the murk ahead, had been only four minutes down on schedule at Huntingdon, ran into the wreckage and was overlaid by splintered remains of its own coaches. A death-roll of 14 resulted.

It turned out that signal wires had been weighed down by wet snow and the formation of ice; one signal arm had needed a 36lb chair to pull it to 'danger'. Signalmen who had seen trains flash past their boxes had checked from their frames that the signals ought to have brought the trains to a stand. There were several lessons to be learned; that fog signalmen should be brought out in conditions of falling snow and that with poor visibility high speeds perhaps ought to be discouraged. The Board of Trade report commented on the 'normal clear' method of block working and the acceptance of expresses right up to the point where shunting was in progress. The Great Northern answer to the false signal indications was to abandon slotted posts and to adopt the centre-pivoted arm or somersault signal which would balance about its centre if loaded with snow or ice. Fail-safe balance weights which would restore an arm to the stop position in most emergencies were the answer on most railways.

In the late summer of 1863 the daring concept of Joseph Mitchell, of a direct main line between Perth and Inverness over the Grampians, was brought into use and was soon part of the new amalgamation, the Highland Railway. It crossed two notable summits, Dava at 1,052ft above sea level, and Druimuachdar Pass at 1,484ft, the highest main-line railway in the British Isles. It took only until February 1865 for it to be seen what drifting could do in the wild Badenoch country between the Forest of Atholl and Strath Spey; the line was closed for five days and reopened only after much toil and sweat. Snow fences, made of sleeper stockades, were hurriedly erected and when the supply of sleepers ran out, plate-layers were drafted to build earth banks to protect the worst affected places. Fences mitigated the problem through many a snowstorm, but some places have always retained their evil reputation, as for example, the 'black tank' as trainmen called a cutting near the head of Glen Garry, where engines settled down for the six-mile slog at 1 in 70 towards the top of the pass. It was improved when the line was doubled, but it continues to be forbidding as the writer realised in comparatively recent times when two black Staniers at the front faltered in a spring snowstorm after dusk had fallen, even going *downhill.*

When William Stroudley became locomotive superintendent of the Highland later in 1865 he devised a comprehensive scheme of snow clearance. Small ploughs were fitted to the buffer beams of many train engines at the onset of winter; they were similar to a cowcatcher and could dispose of drifts up to 2ft in depth. Larger ploughs were used for drifts up to 5ft and were fixed to engines that acted as pilots to train engines after the weather signals from stationmasters had included the ominous 'heavy snow; wind rising' bulletin or 'bad drifts; trains should be piloted and loads reduced'. The largest type of wedge plough, as high as the engine chimney, was used when deeper drifts were likely to be encountered; the big ploughs derived their thrust from three or four engines coupled together. In deep drifts wet snow consolidates into ice, and if this results in

derailment of the plough engines, there follows the tremendously hard task of lifting them on to the track again, usually with jacks since such incidents always seem to happen on single lines or when the crane cannot be brought up through the snow on a parallel track.

Deep drifts in cuttings might need hand removal by relays of gangs lifting the snow away from the track or attacking solid ice with pick and shovel. In the North of Scotland storms often continue so that three days' clearance work is obliterated in a single night. In the Caithness moors, 'the country of the snow drifts', trains have occasionally been buried in drifts and further falls of snow. Dava summit was also notorious for prolonged snow blocks. Passengers who have to seek the shelter of a wayside station in remote sparsely populated places are sometimes far less comfortable than in the train, but somewhere near Dava in 1880 cattle which had refused to be liberated into soft snow from a train stuck at the height of a blizzard stayed in the wagons and were suffocated.

Extraordinary as it might seem, the North British Railway took no heed of the Highland's remedies when it became responsible for operating the West Highland main line, up past Ben Lomond, over the wild expanse of the Moor of Rannoch and by way of Loch Treig to Fort William. The line opened in August 1894 and the very first winter found it a shambles under the stress of frost and driving snow. Only then, after innumerable delays to trains, some lasting several days, many derailments, and snowploughs having to be extricated from drifts by gangs of anything up to 50 men (when they could be transported to the danger spots) was the designing of snow fences embarked upon; Cruach Rock cutting actually received a snow shed of wood and corrugated iron. Today British Railways has gone one better on the

Right: Snow can be a problem even in Turkey, as this shot of a 2-10-0 locomotive near Istanbul shows. *P B Whitehouse*

Dingwall and Skye line, beside Loch Carron, with a concrete structure which should be avalanche proof. On several exposed places Howie snow blowers have proved their worth; close-boarded fencing is laid on each side of the track to make a trough and the force of the gale tends to lift snow clear of the metals.

In countries where snow is a permanent feature of the winter landscape the precautions needful in Britain can be seen on an extended scale. Snow fences and snow sheds became elongated — one stretch on the Central Pacific in the Sierra Nevada range in California scored an early record with a snowshed 30 miles long. More plough power is provided — there is a well-known picture of seven locomotives bucking a drift with a wedge plough near the summit of the Central Pacific — and then a genius named Leslie brightened the 1880s by designing a rotary plough. Today sophisticated rotary ploughs independently powered by steam or diesel engines, so that even on electric railways they are not dependent on current in case snow brings the overhead down, are used wherever snow is dry enough not to be converted into ice by the impact of the blower blades and where a stream of slush can be shot to either side of the track with impunity. Another obviously desirable condition for rotary ploughing is that the snow should not have brought too much rock down from the sides of cuttings. It still remains true, whatever tools are employed in snow clearance, that success depends on the integrity and tough determination of the men who use them.

Much of the art of keeping a railway going in severe weather depends on attention to small detail. Rule 86 requires signalmen to work their signals and points frequently during severe frost or falls of snow when the line is clear to prevent the frost or snow impeding their free working. At this end of the twentieth century we make sure of it with butane gas point heaters of which British Railways has several thousand. Today colour-light signals and enclosed cabs of diesel or electric locomotives have combined to ease the driver's lot in fog or snow; the automatic warning system improves the chances of a driver knowing the true state of a distant signal even when his view is obscured. At least two Scottish accidents — Elliot Junction and Castlecary — which took place in failing light and falling snow might have been avoided if some sort of cab indication had existed, although, as usual with railway accidents, several people as well as vile weather contributed to eventual disaster.

Although overhead conductors on electric railways are less liable to failure than conductor rails in snow, wet snow and ice formation has at times brought them down. For conductor-rail railways reliance is placed on anti-freeze, distributed from baths on the London Underground surface lines or by special spray trains on British Railways. Sleet brushes and ice-breaking collector shoes serve obvious purposes and London Transport on several routes short-circuits the conductor rails, forming in effect giant heating elements, to heat them before train service begins when sleet or snow is forecast. Nature can occasionally defeat man's ingenuity, however, as on the day when warm rain washed the anti-freeze solution off Southern Region third rails and was followed up at once by a fall of sleet which froze to make an insulating layer of ice. By and large, railways at home or abroad are now less liable to be defeated by winter weather than of yore but snowfalls still call for extra vigilance if they are to be safely overcome.

Training a Driver

IN FEW OTHER countries in the world, probably, was there in steam days so little systematic education of engine crews as in Great Britain. There was no royal road to the position of command on the locomotive footplate; the road was a lengthy one, and there were no short cuts. Until after the second world war, however, there were plenty of young men with railways in their blood who were prepared to face all that was involved in a locomotive career. They were destined to learn that all the knowledge they would need ultimately as drivers

inspector would put him through an oral examination, and if by then he showed himself reasonably competent, he would become a 'passed cleaner' — that is, a cleaner who could be called on at any time for a firing duty. Soon after that he would begin regular firing duty.

As a fireman he would have to use his powers of observation to a wider extent than before. Not only would he need to watch how his driver handled the locomotive, but he would require to learn all about the lines over which he worked — the location of signals and stations, the gradients, the speed restrictions for curves, and what the book of rules and regulations had to say

Left: Typical cab view of a four-track line with overhead electrification. D N Jamieson

Below: Rather spartan conditions at the controls of BR Southern Region's early electric mus. British Railways SR

would be picked up more as the result of their own observation than by any systematic instruction.

The driver-to-be had to enter the service, generally in his teens, as a cleaner at one of the sheds or depots at which numbers of locomotives were stationed. During his work of cleaning he would become familiar with the mechanism of the locomotives, as well as of their internal arrangement — he might have to insert himself from to time into an engine's firebox, for example — acquiring the rudiments of knowledge which he would require on the next stage of his career, that of firing. It would be difficult to describe cleaning as a pleasant occupation; the cleaner himself led a life that was very far from clean, and his hours, by day or night according to the locomotive demands, could be very irregular. But until after World War II, as emphasised already, there was no shortage of entrants as cleaners to the railway service.

Probably during the summer season, with its extra trains, or over the rush of a Christmas or Easter weekend, the cleaner would get his first experience of attending the fire of a steam locomotive. It might be on nothing more exciting than a shunting engine, but it would be a welcome change, and would bring its first vision of the future. As to how to fire, the learner fireman would be very dependent on his driver for advice; and the driver might be helpful or the reverse, according to his temperament. In either event, the cleaner would have to use his powers of observation to pick up the knowledge needed for the regular task of firing that lay ahead. In course of time a locomotive

about the safe working of the trains and how to proceed in an emergency. With his increasing knowledge of the road he would learn when his driver required more steam — as when climbing — and when matters could be taken more easily, and he would fire accordingly. Too little firing on the harder stretches might result in lost time, and too much on the easy stretches would mean steam blowing to waste through the safety-valves. Eventually specific drivers and firemen would get paired together, and if their relationship was good, they could become a first-class team, much to the advantage of the fireman's acquisition of knowledge.

So the day would arrive when, after another oral examination, probably by a chief locomotive inspector (himself formerly a driver) our recruit would become a 'passed fireman', authorised to drive. At first, once again, there would be occasional spells of driving at times of pressure, but then our fireman would begin regular driving, working up by degrees through shunting, freight working or slow passenger working, usually after many years, to the coveted 'top link' at his shed, charged with the most responsible and the most remunerative duties. From time to time all engine-crews would have locomotive inspectors riding with them, especially if they were manning engines which in various ways might be proving troublesome. Even so, it has always been axiomatic in British steam locomotive work that an inspector on the footplate can act in no more than an advisory capacity; the actual handling of the engine must remain the driver's responsibility.

In the later years of steam locomotive development in

Sir William Orpen's painting 'The Enginemen of the Night Mail'.
British Transport Museum (B Sharpe)

Great Britain, the need for more formal instruction was beginning to gain recognition. A certain amount of specific tuition started to be given to younger members of the shed staff in specially equipped instruction cars or rooms. So-called mutual improvement classes also provided means of acquiring information, though attendance at them was voluntary. As previously stressed, the major proportion of the British steam locomotive driver's knowledge was amassed casually by personal observation. As a consequence driving standards, and hence locomotive performance, varied widely. Some locomotive men undoubtedly became highly competent, and it has not been unknown for their observations on performance to have influenced locomotive designers. But training methods were casual in the extreme, engendering by no means insignificant losses in efficiency of motive power utilisation.

In the matter of crew training French practice has been well ahead of British. The French driver-to-be had to pass an examination before entering a railway technical school, there to be taught mathematics and science, intermingled with workshop experience and practical work on locomotives. After three years so spent and successfully taking another examination, the *apprenti* had further practical training as a fitter, boiler-maker or machinist until being called up for compulsory military service. On return to the railway he would begin a period as a *chauffeur* or fireman lasting two to three years at the end of which came a very stiff examination in the construction, handling and maintenance of locomotives, and knowledge of signalling, railway operation in general and safety-rules.

Success in the examination earned the title *eleve mecanicien,* or pupil driver. Then would follow three or four years of driving freight or local passenger trains, whereafter success in a final examination would ensure promotion to the position of *mecanicien,* or driver. In French steam locomotive work seniority counted for very little; men with high initial qualifications could be passed through the firing and pupil driver stages much more quickly, with the result that highly capable young drivers might have as their firemen men considerably older than themselves.

In addition, French locomotive handling has always been subject to extremely strict rules. Cab fittings include self-recording speed indicators, the tapes from which show whether or not speed limits have been observed, and whether or not, on approaching a speed restriction or a signal at caution or danger, the driver has acknowledged it by pressing a 'vigilance button', so marking the tape and confirming that he has been fully awake. French engine-crews have also been awarded substantial inducements to drive and fire intelligently, to get the best out of their equipment. One is a bonus for recovering lost time (with the speed recorder to confirm that it was not done by scamping speed restrictions), and another is a bonus for fuel economy (to ensure that the time regained was not at the expense of thrashing the locomotive). In these and other ways French steam locomotive handling, and with it punctuality of operation, reached a higher level probably than anywhere else in the world.

As mentioned earlier, the rather casual methods of recruiting and training locomotive staff continued in Britain until World War II. After conclusion of the war there was a radical change. With so much other employment available offering regular hours in clean shops, and, in general, better pay, locomotive cleaning as the only possible entry to the footplate no longer offered any attraction to the majority of young men; recruitment became increasingly difficult and, in industrial districts, almost impossible. The position was made worse by the very poor condition of the locomotives caused by wartime arrears of maintenance, as also of the locomotive sheds. Electrification would have helped to solve the problem, but even if it could have been financed on a large scale, which at that time was impossible, it would have taken years to carry out (as eventually it did, with the London Midland Region main line out of Euston) and other measures were necessary.

The solution selected, with experience in the United States as an encouragement, was a rapid and wholesale replacement of steam by diesel traction. From 1955 onwards large-scale orders were placed by British Railways for diesel-electric and diesel-hydraulic locomotives and diesel-mechanical multiple-unit train sets. The sheer scale of the requirements meant that some of the order went to builders with relatively little diesel experience as well as to those with adequate qualifications. As a result, diesels of too many different types were introduced, and in the early stages of the changeover troubles were frequent and often severe.

By no means all the troubles were due to design or construction deficiencies. A prime cause was undoubtedly bad and inexperienced handling of the new equipment. In time it became clear that both locomotive men and maintenance staffs had to be trained in techniques suitable to the operation of precision-engineered machines rather than the casual picking up of enough knowledge to get by merely from observation. The establishment of an organisation for the systematic instruction of staff in the design and handling of the new complex machines was complicated by the variety of motive power equipment introduced in a very short time, but gradually fully equipped diesel schools were set up at various strategic centres and the formal training of locomotivemen was belatedly introduced on British Railways.

Naturally enough, some of the older men, imbued with the traditions of steam, found the switch far from easy; it says a good deal for their receptiveness and teaching standards that the very rapid changeover was accomplished with no worse troubles than were actually experienced. Eventually, it need hardly be added, most of the men found the change from the noise, vibration and dirt of a steam locomotive footplate to the relative comfort of a diesel cab very welcome.

Driving an electric train, relieved of the problem of understanding and controlling a primary power unit, has always posed fewer problems. On suburban lines, of course, driving multiple-unit electric sets had been a commonplace for many years; the expertise needed is little more than the movement of two simple controllers for traction and braking, keeping an eye, or an ear open for malfunction warnings, and strict attention to signalling generally of a more complex kind than that in the open country.

Driving main-line electric locomotives is rather a different matter and the equipment of the new

anywhere in Europe. There are reasons for such thoroughness in a country like Switzerland, especially on the lines through the mountains, with continuous gradients of 1 in 37 to 40, constant curvature, heavy trains worked by locomotives of up to 6,500hp, the use of regenerative braking to control the speeds on the long down-grades, and other conditions calling for a high degree of driving skill and intelligence.

The entrant to the service must be a Swiss citizen of between 20 and 30 years, not less than 5ft 3in tall, and he must have had at least five years previous experience as a fitter or a mechanic. His first 300 days are spent in the maintenance of locomotives at one of the principal depots, during which he will pass through nine courses in the design of motive power units. Then follow a second 300 days as an assistant driver on a locomotive, passing through eight courses on the rules of operation and

Driver under instruction on the realistic electric locomotive simulator at Willesden. *British Railways LMR*

high-power ac electric loco-motives for the rebuilt London Midland Region's main line was more complicated than that of previous electric traction units. Apart from that, main-line electric locomotive drivers had to become accustomed to working their trains at 100mph speeds, which, even with the safeguard of the automatic warning system, required more concentrated attention to the road ahead than ever before.

For training drivers of the new locomotives British Railways installed at Willesden a most elaborate simulator training unit. The trainee sits in the driving position in a mock-up of an electric locomotive cab, complete with normal controls, looking through the cab front window at a filmed representation of a journey at high speed. The equipment can be made to simulate all normal responses to conditions and driver handling, as well as a variety of emergencies, thus providing a very realistic means of comprehensive driver training before venturing forth with a real locomotive on a real track.

Possibly the Swiss have developed the most complete system of training for electric train drivers to be found

signalling, followed by an examination extending over two days.

There is then a third 300 days, still as an assistant driver, with four instruction courses on a driver's duties, leading to a first examination, which includes two days spent in theoretical tests. Then comes a 30-day period in which the trainee takes charge of a locomotive for the first time, under the eye of an experienced supervisor. Two days' practical examination in driving follow, after which the driver-to-be is authorised to drive on his own, but still at an assistant driver's rate of pay, until at the end of a final 300 days there comes a very thorough final driver's examination. If this is passed to satisfaction, appointment as a fully qualified driver follows at the full rate of pay.

Not surprisingly, after four years of training, preceded by the required five years experience as a fitter or a mechanic, driving in Switzerland is a well-paid occupation, as indeed it should be. The fully qualified driver not only has his extensive driving experience, but also sufficient experience to correct any minor fault that might occur on a locomotive during the course of a run. As a result, a locomotive breakdown in Switzerland is a very rare occurrence.

Inside a Diesel Locomotive Depot

B.R. Warship and Hymek diesel-hydraulic locomotives at Bristol Bath Road depot.

G R Hounsell

A MAJOR ECONOMY resulting from the replacement of steam by diesel traction is that it permits a drastic reduction in motive power maintenance and servicing facilities. This is because, with its greater fuel capacity and less frequent servicing requirements, the diesel locomotive can be operated more continuously than a steam engine, and can therefore be diagrammed to work much higher mileages between depot visits. As fewer units are required in traffic to perform an equivalent amount of work, and since operating can be extended over greater distances, minor depots and sub-sheds can be dispensed with, and all servicing and maintenance concentrated at a few strategically sited major depots which may be anything from 50 to 100 miles apart.

As an example, the Western Region of British Railways, which relies entirely on diesel power, has replaced a total of over 60 steam depots (excluding sub-sheds) with only six main depots with maintenance and servicing facilities and nine servicing points. The servicing points are depots without the facilities to carry out extensive repairs.

During the first phase of diesel working, when all maintenance and servicing had to be carried out in existing steam depots, it soon became evident that such conditions were quite inadequate and that to achieve anything like optimum efficiency a new type of motive power depot designed to meet the specific requirements of diesel traction was imperative.

Fortunately it was possible to draw generally on the extensive diesel experience of American railroads and, in particular, on the first example of a modern diesel depot in this country, which had been installed by the Steel Company of Wales at its Abbey Works, Port Talbot in 1955. Although designed for the maintenance and servicing of shunting locomotives, this depot had been lavishly equipped and planned in a manner that was equally well adapted for line service locomotives. It proved an excellent prototype and many of its main features were subsequently adopted as standard practice by British Rail.

The most notable difference between the type of diesel depot evolved by BR and the old steam shed is the emphasis on preventive maintenance, which is now carried out in specially designed workshops in accordance with predetermined schedules — whereas in steam days it was done very much on an ad hoc basis — as and when required, and then often in some available corner of the running shed. Today the maintenance block is the principal feature of a diesel depot; it consists of a main shed which houses the locomotives and a number of subsidiary workshops, stores and premises for staff amenities. As a rule the main building contains from three to five tracks, with pits beneath, set about 15ft apart and providing examination and repair berths for up to about a dozen main-line locomotives.

The principal feature of the general design is the provision of three working levels, arranged to permit the maximum degree of access to all parts of the locomotive. The lowest working level is in the pits between the rails, which allows work to be carried out on the traction motors, brakes and other underside equipment. The concrete floor is usually rather more than four feet

below rail level in order to provide sufficient headroom, and for general cleanliness the sides are faced with glazed tiles. Lighting is provided by fluorescent panels flush-mounted at suitable intervals in the side walls, and access is by a short flight of steps at each end.

The middle working level is provided in the space between the tracks which forms the main shop floor. The tracks themselves are raised about 2ft 6in above the general floor level to give a convenient height for working on the springs, bogies, brake gear and other equipment mounted externally below the footplating. Access to this level is usually by means of a short ramp to facilitate the movement of mobile equipment.

The top level takes the form of a continuous concrete platform or decking on a level with the footplating of the locomotives, supported from the floor by concrete posts. The platforms give access to the diesel engine, generators, batteries, cab and all other equipment above the running plate. It is in effect the principal working area and is at the same level as the various ancillary workshops for battery attention, coach repairs, riggers, welding, electrical testing, general fitting and general stores, to give direct access to this level and avoid the effort of running up and down stairs.

All the maintenance bays engaged on major overhaul and repair work are spanned by overhead gantry cranes — usually one at each end of the shop — to carry out the replacement of heavy parts, such as engines and

Left, above and right: Five pictures showing various servicing activities in BR motive power depots; the one immediately above shows both diesel and electric locomotives at Reddish depot. *All British Railways*

generators. Where the platforms are continuous this requires the provision of removable metal grilles in the decks so that the parts can be raised and lowered through them to the ground floor level.

Another essential requirement is to equip one track with a set of synchronised lifting jacks capable of raising locomotives so that the bogies and springs can be removed for changing or cleaning. In addition this track is usually fitted with locomotive weighing equipment. Outside the shop is a heavy-duty hoist to lift the bogies on and off rail wagons used to transport them to and from the bogie shop.

A number of electric power and compressed-air points for operating various tools and equipment are dispersed throughout the shop. There are also conveniently placed dispensing points for fresh lubricating oils, steam and water, and similar points to which pipes are coupled for the drainage of dirty oil from the engines to a collecting tank outside the shed, and for the dispersal of steam from the train heating boilers to the atmosphere.

Where the maintenance shop layout consists of bays at each end, as illustrated in the drawing the central area is used as a working or storage space, with direct access to an adjacent section housing offices, stores, canteen, mess rooms, staff amenities and ancillary workshops. Many types of engineering are catered for in the ancillary workshops, including a general shop for the cleaning and adjustment of engine parts, equipped with drills, sanders, saws, wire brushing machines and valve grinders; there are also fuel pump- and injector-testing and air equipment rooms, a battery-charging room where batteries are periodically serviced, and if suspect, stripped and rebuilt, an electrical shop where control gear, contactors, relays, automatic voltage regulators, dynamos and alternators are dealt with, and welders and coachbuilders shops. There is also a large stores department holding supplies of special-purpose tools and stocks of several thousand electrical and mechanical spare parts.

Fume extraction equipment consists of electrically driven fans supplemented by pneumatically controlled air inlet louvres built into the walls to maintain a through flow of fresh air. Depot interior lighting is mainly flourescent strip, and there is also a 110 volt supply to feed the electric circuits of the locomotives. Electric power socket outlets are provided at the locomotive berths for the connection of welding plant, battery chargers, tools etc. Space heating is usually by means of an automatic high-pressure hot-water system burning waste engine oil in a central boiler.

To save expense many diesel maintenance shops have been adapted from existing buildings, but where they are of new construction the main structure is of steel and concrete with extensive glazing in both the walls and roof to provide maximum natural lighting. In sharp contrast to the dark and cramped conditions that characterised so many of the old steam workshops, their bright well-designed modern interiors rank them among the best examples of industrial architecture in Britain today.

Perhaps the greatest difference between past and present practice is that nowadays the Depot Master of a maintenance shed is not concerned with the employment of his locomotives nor the engine crews that man them. His responsibility is simply to supply the Movements Officer with reliable locomotives. The

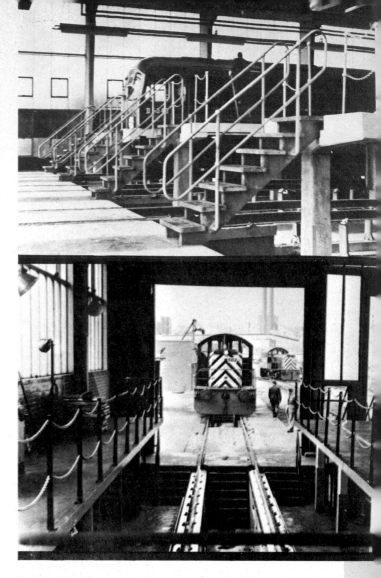

day-to-day allocation of locomotives to work diagrams is the responsibility of the Diesel Locomotive Controller, with the proviso that the depot is supplied with accurate information concerning the mileage and engine hours needed to determine a unit's maintenance requirements. At the end of each week the data thus obtained is entered on each locomotive's individual record card so that its next scheduled maintenance period can be readily ascertained and provided for. On some railways the running information is fed to a central computer which does the calculations and issues notice when a schedule examination is approaching. British Railways is at present installing such a computer system.

The whole system of diesel maintenance is based on predetermined hourly periods in service — the specified work being carried out at scheduled intervals in accordance with the requirements of the type of locomotives concerned. For example, on the Western Region of BR a general examination check-up is carried out every 125 engine running hours, and these routine inspections coincide with more important maintenance carried out at intervals of 750, 1,500, 3,000, 6,000 and 12,000 engine hours.

High-speed diesel engines need a complete overhaul every 6,000 hours, which entails the removal of the engine for dispatch to the main locomotive works for attention. In the meantime the locomotive is fitted with a replacement engine fresh from overhaul. This system of unit replacement is especially useful for dealing with major components as it cuts to a minimum the time that the locomotive is out of traffic.

Repairs to major locomotive components come under four categories, namely, unscheduled, light attention,

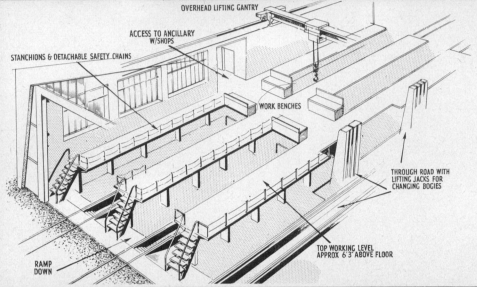

Left: The four illustrations show various aspects of the three working levels in a modern diesel maintenance depot; the photo above left is of the Steel Company of Wales prototype layout at Port Talbot. *All P F Winding*

Below: General layout of the BR Western Region Canton depot at Cardiff. *P F Winding*

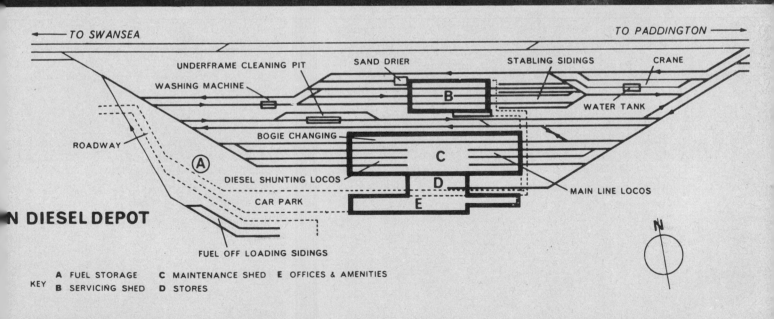

N DIESEL DEPOT

KEY
A FUEL STORAGE   C MAINTENANCE SHED   E OFFICES & AMENITIES
B SERVICING SHED   D STORES

intermediate and general. Light attention covers such items as fitting a new engine turbocharger, or tyre-turning on a ground lathe without removing the bogies. Intermediate repairs apply primarily to bodies, engines and transmissions. A general overhaul (every 12,000 hours in the case of line- service locomotives with medium-speed diesel engines) is given approximately every five years and entails a visit to the main works, where in addition to a rebuilt engine it will probably have a body overhaul at the same time.

Unscheduled repairs occur as a result of accidents and locomotive failures, and part of a depot's capacity must always be held in reserve for such occurrences to avoid interfering with scheduled maintenance. Other suspected faults such as axle flaws and fractured castings might require a whole class of locomotives to be called in for examination at short notice, so that even with carefully controlled planning disruptions are not always avoidable.

Although diesel maintenance depots differ in layout, they are all basically alike in having the same components, and Fig 2 illustrates a typical arrangement at the Canton depot of the Western Region at Cardiff. The key position and size of the maintenance shop clearly indicates its importance, while immediately to the north is the servicing shed, which provides facilities for the daily inspection, servicing and fuelling of locomotives in traffic as distinct from those undergoing maintenance. Servicing sheds deal with any locomotive regardless of its allocation and their accommodation consists of a simple shed with sufficient berths to stand the maximum number of locomotives requiring simultaneous attention.

inspection to detect loose, leaking or defective parts, and with the engine running or the locomotive moving, checks are made on brakes and deadman's apparatus, windscreen wipers, sanding gear, auxiliary generator voltage and battery charging. A sample of the engine sump oil is taken with the engine running to establish the approximate percentage of fuel dilution, content of water, and content of insoluble solids in the sampe. Should any tests show that the allowable amount of contamination has been reached, the lubricating oil is partially or completely changed.

A BR Class 35 Hymek diesel-hydraulic locomotive at Gloucester depot in February 1970. *N E Preedy*

Like many other servicing sheds, the one at Canton has been adapted from the original steam shed, the main alteration being that the number of engine roads is reduced so that the available width between them is sufficiently increased to allow for the installation of fuelling points and other servicing equipment. This reduces the number of locomotive berths to about a dozen, but even for a depot with an allocation of over a hundred engines this is more than adequate because, unlike the steam engine, which once the fires are dropped requires a lengthy period of servicing, diesel locomotives can be dealt with almost as rapidly as road vehicles.

Apart from fuel and water points a servicing shed also requires a compressed-air system for power greasing and the topping up of lubricating oils and engine coolant at each berth. Exhaust steam pipes are also provided at convenient points to allow steam generated during the routine testing of train heating boilers to be discharged through the roof. There are inspection pits to each road with fluorescent lighting to facilitate inspection, and some sheds also have lowered sidewalks and platforms at footplate level. With diesel locomotives a thorough daily routine examination is essential, since even a minor fault if undetected, can easily result in a total failure of the locomotive in traffic.

The routine examinations consist of a general visual

Other depot equipment includes a sand drier with oil-fired heating in the immediate vicinity of the servicing shed or, where metallic grit is used, a gravity feed to the locomotives from overhead hoppers. Also in the yard and usually sited on an approach road to the servicing shed there is usually a two-stage automatic washing machine, in which the first stage is a detergent-solution application and the second a water wash. The machinery is brought into position when a locomotive approaching the wash intercepts the beam of a photo-electric cell; the duration of each application is governed by a time-switch. In addition to body cleansing plant many depots have an underframe cleaning plant employing either steam or hot water jets.

With the changeover from coal to oil, depot fuelling arrangements have also undergone a complete transformation. Open coal trucks have given place to tank wagons which discharge directly into big diesel oil storage tanks, from where it is distributed through pipes to the locomotive fuelling points in the servicing area. Fuel oil has also eliminated the problem of ash disposal, and such waste as there is from sump oil can now be usefully employed for fuelling the oil-fired boilers of the depot heating system.

The overall picture that emerges by comparison with steam traction is one of much higher productivity, cleaner methods and a big saving in labour requirements.

BRITISH RAIL
IN PICTURES

Top: English Electric Type 3 Co-Co diesel-electric No D6894 leaving Sunderland with empty coal wagons in August 1967. *B Stephenson*

Left: English Electric Type 1 Bo-Bo No D8127 passing Shap village with empty hoppers from Carlisle to Shap quarry in April 1967. *B Stephenson*

Bottom: British Rail's experimental gas-turbine-powered APT (advanced passenger train) at the Derby Railway Technical Centre. *British Transport Films*

Above: BR Class 86 ac electric locomotive at full blast on the LMR main line at Berkhamsted. *British Transport Films*

Above right: Unusual combination of 2HAP and 4CIG dc electric mu sets forming a Victoria-Portsmouth train on the SR mid-Sussex line. *British Transport Films*

Right: BR experimental 4PEP sliding-door emu for high-density service, at Shepperton. *J A Bingham*

Far right above: SR 4SUB emu set forming a Victoria-Beckenham Junction train, at Crystal Palace. *B Stephenson*

Below right: Diesel mu set on the LMR Keswick-Penrith line (now closed) at Threlkeld. *C Lees*

Below: Arundel castle forming a backdrop to a SR 4CEP emu on the mid-Sussex line. *British Transport Films*

RAILWAY ODDITIES

Compensating Rod Drives

FOR THE SAKE OF convenience, articulated locomotives may be divided into two categories. There are those in which the cylinders and driving mechanism are part of the mobile unit and share in its movement; and those where the cylinders are attached to the main frames, with a driving mechanism arranged to allow for the displacement of the moving trucks.

The second type mentioned avoids the disadvantage of flexible steam pipes, but it necessarily requires a more complicated driving system – as can be seen in the accompanying illustration which is based on a design built for the 760mm-gauge Bosnia-Herzegovina Railway by the well-known Austrian firm of Krauss.

In this example, the engine is carried by two closely spaced bogies giving an extremely short rigid wheelbase. The cylinders are rigidly attached to the main frame and drive through rods and rocking beams whose fulcrums are also secured to the main frames. It will be apparent that since the stroke from the rockers is constant, a

means must be provided to allow for the virtual lengthening and shortening required of the final drive rods as the wheels assume varying angular positions in relation to the main frames, so that the bogies can move in conformity with track curvature.

The required compensation is achieved by taking the drive through crossbeams which pivot on the main frame, and thence through rods each side connected to bell-cranks carried on floating bearings concentric with the rocking beam pivots. The horizontal arms of the bell-cranks are connected by links to a lower pair of rectangular bell-cranks, from which short vertical arms transmit the final drive by connecting rods to the wheels.

In theory, a big advantage of the type of engine described is that it requires only two cylinders instead of the four that would be necessary if the cylinders were combined directly with the flexibly mounted trucks. In practice the advantage is far outweighed by the clumsy and complicated driving system, which apart from being an engineer's nightmare, limited the engine to relatively low working speeds.

Nevertheless locomotives articulated by compensating rod-work enjoyed quite a vogue in the Balkans, where it is likely that the low speeds enforced by the difficult terrain afforded them a greater measure of success than would normally be expected.

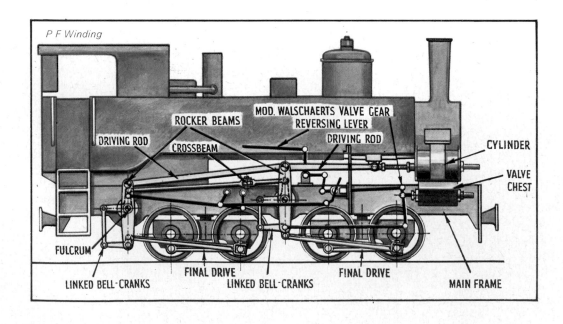

P F Winding

ROCKER BEAMS · DRIVING ROD · CROSSBEAM · MOD. WALSCHAERTS VALVE GEAR REVERSING LEVER · DRIVING ROD · CYLINDER · VALVE CHEST · FULCRUM · LINKED BELL-CRANKS · FINAL DRIVE · LINKED BELL-CRANKS · FINAL DRIVE · MAIN FRAME

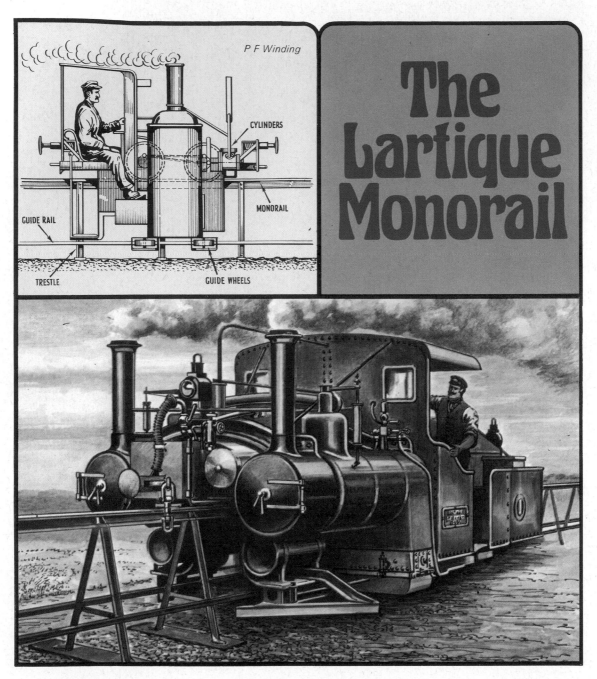

P F Winding

CYLINDERS

MONORAIL

GUIDE RAIL

TRESTLE

GUIDE WHEELS

The Lartigue Monorail

TODAY THE Lartigue monorail system is mainly remembered in conjunction with the Listowel and Ballybunion Railway, which despite having been dismantled about fifty years ago, is still popularly referred to in Ireland as the Monorail.

Originally Lartigue's idea was said to have been inspired by the sight of a camel train in Algeria, with the heavy laden animals balanced by panniers on each side. On a similar principle, he devised a system using a single rail supported on a row of triangular trestles, with the vehicles centred on the rail; the two halves of the vehicles, one on each side of the trestle, were stabilised by small transverse wheels which engaged a light guide rail fixed to each side of the trestle.

In its early simple form, the system proved useful on plantations and mineral workings, where its cheap construction, and the ease with which it could be dismantled and re-erected, gave it a distinct advantage in temporary situations and over rough ground, because no roadbed was required.

In 1886 Lartigue decided to carry the idea a stage further and to challenge the supremacy of the narrow-gauge railways which were then at the height of

their popularity. Accordingly, he demonstrated his system in London, using a small steam motive unit with twin vertical boilers. The driver sat astride the monorail on a seat mounted behind the boilers (smaller illustration) in what must have been a decidely uncomfortable position.

The demonstration aroused considerable interest, and prompted the promoters to spend a further £30,000 in mounting the Ballybunion project, which was to provide a public railway linking the seaside resort with the existing main-line railhead at Listowel – a distance of 9½ miles.

In the event, it turned out to be a disastrous mistake, because no one had foreseen the complexities involved in applying the system to the carriage of passengers and general merchandise, as opposed to the private handling of a single commodity. The problems were innumerable, and it says much for the ingenuity of the promoters and the tolerance of the Irish that the line managed to survive for 36 years. Although it failed completely in its first object – to promote monorails – it at least achieved a certain immortality in the great tradition of Irish humour.

Steam Tram Engines

ALTHOUGH THE steam tram engine was pioneered in Britain, it never achieved the success here that it did on the Continent. Originally introduced in the 1870s as a substitute for horse traction on urban tramways, it was exported in considerable numbers by such firms as Merryweather, Kitson and Beyer Peacock until European builders eventually managed to supply their own markets.

In Britain progress was dogged from the start by public opposition to the smoke and noise, and also because, it was objected, that even with totally enclosed motion the tram engines frightened horses. In London, where they began running in 1883, hostility was so great they they never got far beyond the Tottenham district, and were eventually withdrawn in favour of horse traction some years prior to the start of electric working.

Their most favourable development was in the Birmingham and South Staffordshire districts between 1882-1888, and at one time the City of Birmingham Tramways Company owned 102 steam engines — the largest fleet in the country. But even there they were soon replaced by electric traction, and all had disappeared by 1907. But although electrification soon dismissed the steam tram from all but a few remote rural areas in Britain, the position on the Continent was rather different. There, in the more populated areas inter-urban tramway development far exceeded anything in Britain,

and on those unelectrified semi-rural lines the tram engine managed to survive well into the middle of the twentieth century.

In Europe tram engines were also used extensively by industry and by minor lines for local trip workings to the nearest main-line railhead. But whatever their origin the vast majority of tram engines shared a remarkable uniformity in that they were mostly of the 0-4-0 wheel arrangement, with two cylinders an enclosed boiler and enclosed motion beneath the running plate. Our drawing of a standard Kitson engine, as used on the Leeds-Headingly line until 1904, depicts a typical layout as seen with the bodywork removed.

The standard Kitson engines had outside cylinders arranged as high as possible to be clear of the mud and dust. The valve gear was a modification of Walschaert's, patented by Kitson, using a floating lever linking the crosshead to the valve spindle; intermediately, at a point near the valve spindle; the lever was pinned to the radius link, which received its rocking movement through an arm pinned to the coupling rod. A common feature of tram engines was that only about a third of the exhaust steam went up the chimney, the remainder being dealt with by a condenser on the roof. The weight of the engines in working order was 9-10 tons and the wheelbase was only 4ft 6in.

In Britain the usual practice was for an engine to haul one 60-seat bogie trailer, but on the Continent they often handled up to half a dozen four-wheeled trailers which in peak periods might contain anything up to 500 passengers. In fact, despite its somewhat curious and antiquated appearance, the tram engine at its best was a remarkably lively and powerful machine: considering its diminutive size, it regularly performed prodigious feats when competently handled.

Du Bousquet Tanks

ARTICULATED standard-gauge steam engines have always been something of a rarity in Europe, particularly in Britain and France. Apart from a few prototypes, the only designs of any consequence this century were the 33 Fowler Beyer-Garratts for the LMS, and the du Bousquet 0-6-2 + 2-6-0 compound tanks built for the Nord in 1905 and later adopted by the Ceinture and Est railways. Some du Bousquets were also exported to Spain and China.

The du Bousquet system of articulation is unique in that the main frame comprises a rigid box girder which carries the boiler, the buffing and draw gear at each end, and the whole of the superstructure with the exception of the front water tanks. This central girder rests above the axles and between the frames of the two independent motor bogies, with sufficient clearance to permit adequate movement, and supported by means of pivots — the rear bogie having a flat pivot permitting it to turn on a horizontal axis, and the front bogie a spherical pivot to take up any position caused by the inequalities of the track without affecting the suspended mass resting on the central girder. The reason for mounting the front water tanks directly on the front bogie was to ensure that it remained properly loaded.

P F Winding

CEINTURE   6.007

P F Winding

As was customary on the Nord, the engine was a four-cylinder compound. The low-pressure cylinders were mounted on the front bogie and the high-pressure cylinders on the rear, each pair being interconnected by steam pipes with universal telescopic jointing. The design was originally devised by du Bousquet for handling heavy coal trains of up to 1,000 tons over the difficult gradients in North-east France — a task that previously required the services of two four-cylinder compound 4-6-0s. The du Bousquet developed the same power as two 4-6-0s but weighed only 106 tons and had a relatively light axle load of 15 tons. It could negotiate the severest curves and did not require turntables as it ran equally well in each direction. The only real operating disadvantage was lack of speed, but that was no greater handicap to coal trains, nor on the short-haul transit freights between the mainline marshalling yards around Paris, for which purpose the Ceinture purchased 38 of them between 1909 and 1912 and the Est acquired 13.

Like most complex and unusual machines they were not exactly popular with the enginemen — but whatever their faults they must have been fundamentally sound to have lasted as long as they did. In 1938 the SNCF renumbered the survivors 031-130 TA 1-47 and 031-130 TB 1-12, the latter having been rebuilt with superheaters and piston valves. By 1949 the number in service had dwindled from an original 99 to 29, plus one which had been put aside for preservation. Unfortunately the earmarked engine was inadvertently cut up with the rest, and except in the unlikely event of a survivor in China it must be presumed that this very interesting design is now extinct.

The Fell System

ALTHOUGH IT UTILISED a centre rail to provide ability to climb slopes steeper than could be tackled with simple adhesion, the Fell system was not a rack-and-pinion railway; the centre rail was of a normal bullhead section laid on its side to give two running surfaces, which were engaged by four horizontally mounted auxiliary driving wheels.

The essential feature of the system, patented in 1863 by John Barraclough Fell, was that the horizontal wheels beneath the engine were forced against the centre rail by a powerful screw motion acting on springs, gripping the rail between them. The horizontal wheels driven by the engine thus added their driving force to that of the ordinary vertical driving wheels. All eight driving wheels were coupled in a manner that caused them to revolve together, thus minimising any tendency to slip. When ascending a gradient that was becoming too steep for normal adhesion, the driver operated the control applying pressure to the wheels gripping the centre rail until the adhesion was sufficient to utilise the traction power of the engine without slipping. On descents the same process could be used for braking. On easier sections where they were not required the horizontal wheels could be disengaged from the centre rail.

Preliminary trials carried out on the Cromford and High Peak Railway between 1863 and 1865 on gradients of 1 in 12 were so satisfactory that the French and Italian Governments offered a concession for a 48-mile line to be laid over the public highway across the Mont Cenis pass over the Graian Alps. The line opened in 1867 and operated successsfully for 3½ years, until the opening of the Mont Cenis tunnel made it redundant. The ruling grade on the French side was 1 in 13, where the locomotive, which weighed only 17 tons in working order, was able to handle a trailing load of 16 tons at 11mph, and a maximum of 48 tons at a lower speed. The overall journey time for the 48 miles was just over seven hours, inclusive of stops, and in all about 100,000 passengers and the Italian mail were carried without serious accident.

Despite the early success, the Fell system never gained widespread popularity – possibly because it was only practicable to apply it to small engines of a type that ran only at low speeds. However, it was adopted by the Wairarapa Railway for the route through the Rimutaka mountains in the North Island of New Zealand in 1875. The company had six 0-4-2Ts built for the steep section, designed to take a load of 65 tons up the 1 in 15 incline. Trains of 260 tons were allowed, with four locomotives spaced out along the train. Speeds were low, only 6mph on the way up and 10mph on the descent. The incline continued to replace by a five-mile tunnel.

Possibly the last example of a line using the Fell system is the Snaefell Mountain railway, which is a branch of the Manx Electric Railway in the Isle of Man. The Snaefell is 3ft 6in-gauge line worked by large tramway-type bogie vehicles; the interesting point about it is that the Fell apparatus is not actually required for the ascent of the 2,034ft mountain, but is used only for braking on the way down.

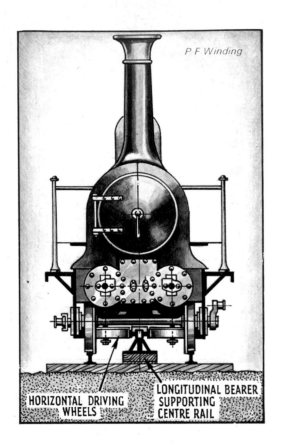

P F Winding

HORIZONTAL DRIVING WHEELS

LONGITUDINAL BEARER SUPPORTING CENTRE RAIL

Crampton's Patents

FIG. 1

P F Winding

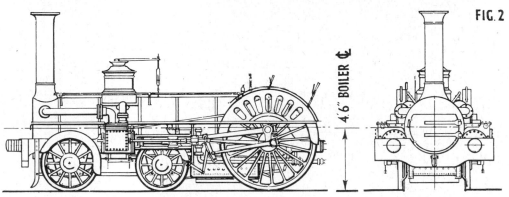

FIG. 2

4' 6" BOILER ℄

LIKE MANY OTHER early locomotive engineers, Thomas Russell Crampton was of the firm opinion that there was no good reason why trains on the standard (or narrow gauge, as it was then called) should not run at the same speeds and with the same steadiness that distinguished the broad gauge. As a young man he worked at Swindon on the design of broad-gauge locomotives at a time when the controversy about the rival merits of the two gauges was at its peak; it was probably that experience that aroused his interest and led eventually to the Crampton patents.

Crampton's theory was that a steady engine would result if the centre of gravity was situated on or near the same horizontal line as the drawbar — a requirement that meant that the boiler had to be pitched much lower than in normal practice. His first patent of 1842 combined two claims. In the first the boiler was slung under the driving axle, while in the second the driving axle was placed behind the firebox.

The sole example of the first claim is shown in Fig 1, the famous *Cornwall* built to the designs of Francis Trevithick for the LNWR in 1847, and shown here in the form that it was displayed at the Great Exhibition of 1851 with the boiler slung beneath the 8ft 6in-diameter driving wheels. Not surprisingly, it did not last long in this state, and was rebuilt as a six-wheeled engine with a

new boiler above the driving axle in 1858. It then ran in regular service until 1902, and thereafter on departmental duties until 1927, when it was finally retired; it is now preserved at the Museum of British Transport at Clapham.

With the second claim (Fig 2) he was more successful. A typical arrangement set the driving axle behind the firebox and the boiler above a pair of rigid carrying axles. Thus the centre line of the boiler could be pitched very low, with the centre of gravity within about a foot of the drawbar. The long wheelbase cylinders mounted near the centre of the engine, were also intended to give steady riding.

Even so, the Cramptons did not prove popular in England and out of a total of 25 built few survived for more than a decade. On the other hand, they were well liked in France and Germany, where a total of nearly 300 was constructed up to 1864. Perhaps they were better suited to the Continental permanent way of that period, and it was only at a later date when train loads increased that their lack of adhesion told against them. Certainly they were fast runners, and as late as the Paris Exhibition of 1889, the highest speed of all the engines tested, 89.5mph, was attained by a single-driver Crampton-type engine with a load of 157½ tons.

Screw - Driven Railway

HEAD of an engineering firm, William Yorath Lewis was one of the many inventors who have devoted themselves to designing a new form of railway. He went to the Paris Exhibition in 1900 and determined to produce something better than the moving pavements used there for transport round the pavilions. His answer was a vehicle to run on solid rubber tyres on concrete tracks, propelled by a jointed screw turning in a central trough. Each carriage was connected to the screw by a rod carrying rollers arranged to engage with the thread of the screw.

With a close pitch of the screw thread, the vehicle ran slowly and with an opened-out thread the speed of the vehicles was increased and they automatically became spaced farther apart. An experimental line was built at Southend Kursaal in 1923 and one ran at Wembley Exhibition in the two following years. At Wembley the speed varied from 1½mph to 12mph, but in later (untried) projects an upper speed limit of 48mph was claimed to be feasible.

The Wembley line was three-quarters of a mile long and at each end a turnstile-like device was arranged to pick the cars off one screw and put them on the thread of that going in the opposite direction. Passengers boarded and alighted at the 10 stations, where the thread was close-pitched and speed was at its lowest; average speed of the line was relatively high.

The constant-speed shaft carrying the spiral thread was driven by 14 electric motors but the 88 24-seat cars constantly moving (or never stopping) were exceptionally economical and used only 170kW an hour. Repair costs also were stated to be minimal. Even so, although schemes were discussed for Lewis Never-Stop passenger lines in Swansea, Berne and Valparaiso, none materialised.

Ship Railways

HISTORY RECORDS that the Greeks used a ship railway for nearly four centuries, for the transport of sea-going vessels across the Isthmus of Corinth, which divides the Aegean and Ionian seas. It is thought to have comprised a causeway of parallel stone blocks into which grooves were cut for the guidance of wheels or rollers which carried the weight of the ship.

Much later, 1438, the same idea was used by the Venetians when 30 galleys were hauled from the Adige to Lake Garda by 1,000 oxen. Subsequently, in 1453, it was used by the Turks to change the course of world history, when they moved their fleet overland into the Golden Horn to bring about the fall of Constantinople.

In Britain, the most important application was on the Bude canal in 1826, where boats attached to endless chains were moved up and down seven inclined planes, supported by small iron wheels on rails. From 1830 similar but more comprehensive schemes were employed in America, notably on the Allegheny Portage Railroad, a 36½-mile line with rope-worked inclines powered by stationary engines, and level sections worked by ordinary locomotives. In 1860 it was proposed that a ship railway should carry vessels at 20mph across the Isthmus of Suez, which it was claimed could be done for one-seventh of the cost of a canal.

Another proposal was for a 112-mile ship railway across the Isthmus of Tehuantepec in Southern Mexico, as an alternative route to the Panama canal.

It was to have loading docks capable of raising vessels of up to 7,000 tons, and a roadbed 50ft wide to accommodate several standard-gauge tracks laid with heavy rail. Gradients were limited to 1 in 100, and it was considered that three articulated locomotives could handle the huge multi-wheel cradle and its load at 10mph.

Surprising as it might seem, this and similar schemes in North America had a lot of official backing, and in Nova Scotia work on one project went on for several years before being abandoned on account of financial difficulties.

The nearest approach to the idea of a ship railway in use today, is the towing of vessels through canals by railborne vehicles. The most impressive example is that of the Panama canal, where ships are moved through the locks by specially equipped double-bogie electric locomotives, called mules.

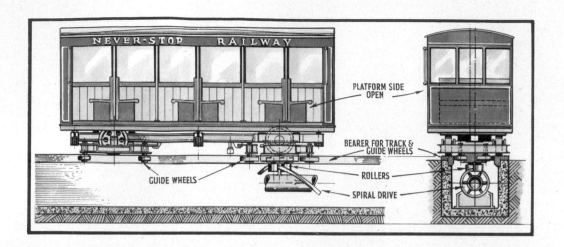

NEVER-STOP RAILWAY

PLATFORM SIDE
OPEN

BEARER FOR TRACK &
GUIDE WHEELS

GUIDE WHEELS

ROLLERS

SPIRAL DRIVE

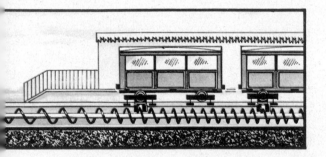

Above: Details of an actual car of the Lewis
Never-Stop railway of 1923. *P F Winding*

Left: Drawing illustrating how the pitch of
the driving screw thread was shortened to
reduce car speed and spacing at boarding
places. *P F Winding*

P F Winding

The Bennie Railplane

THE DESIGN by George Bennie of a high-speed overhead suspended monorail (called the Railplane System of Transport) combined the basic ideas of the well-known Wuppertal Schwebebahn with the work of a German engineer, Dr Otto Stienitz, who claimed that railcars could be driven at high speed by an aircraft engine and propeller. Some years later a propeller-driven vehicle did attain 140mph — but it was on conventional railway track.

Bennie's idea was to use a suspended monorail system in which a lightweight streamlined vehicle was driven by airscrews at each end. The idea was first demonstrated in model form, and again in 1930 by a full-scale vehicle on a 426ft length of track built over a disused spur of the London & North Eastern Railway outside Milngavie, near Glasgow.

The track was in the form of a lattice box girder supported by steel trestles at 80ft intervals. Thus the space beneath the structure was entirely clear, enabling it to be carried above an existing road or railway, as indeed was the case at Milngavie. As may be seen from the illustration, the main running rail was attached to the lattice box girder, while a lighter structure beneath the car carried an auxiliary rail, which controlled the natural inclination of the car to bank on curves by means of guide wheels on short vertical axles.

Each car was electrically driven and could be run singly or in multiple with others. It was claimed that speeds of 200mph could be attained, but of course that could not be demonstrated over the short length of the experimental track.

The braking was through the rails, with shoes arranged to grip both the top and bottom rails; it gave a braking rate about four times higher than normal railway

P F Winding

practice, which might have been most uncomfortable for the passengers. The cab signalling system was very advanced for the time. If the driver ignored a cautionary yellow it automatically changed to red and applied the brakes. The airscrews remained turning all the time, so that when the signal changed to green and released the brakes, the train again moved forward. Thus the trains were claimed to be immune from weather conditions affecting the track or visibility.

Not surprisingly, the Bennie Railplane attracted widespread public interest, and there was no shortage of suggestions as to where it could be profitably employed. One scheme mooted the possibility of London to Paris in 2½ hours — using a seaplane over the Channel, while another with a familiar ring about it was for a line from Heston Airport to London partly over the track of the Great Western Railway. It was also considered as a means of segregating fast from slow traffic by using it over existing railway lines.

But for whatever reasons, none of the schemes ever saw the light of day. Probably the main deterrent was the likely cost of maintaining such an elaborate and vulnerable structure over any considerable distance. Although the demonstration section was of very lightweight construction, it must have been clear enough even to a layman, that the passenger load with single-car trains could never give an economic return, while the use of high-density multiple-units would involve a much greater outlay for a far stronger supporting structure.

Eventually the Milngavie test track was dismantled and sold in 1956.

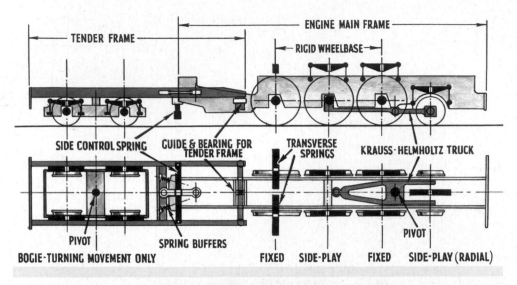

TENDER FRAME · ENGINE MAIN FRAME

RIGID WHEELBASE

SIDE CONTROL SPRING · GUIDE & BEARING FOR TENDER FRAME · TRANSVERSE SPRINGS · KRAUSS-HELMHOLTZ TRUCK

PIVOT · SPRING BUFFERS · PIVOT

BOGIE-TURNING MOVEMENT ONLY · FIXED · SIDE-PLAY · FIXED · SIDE-PLAY (RADIAL)

P F Winding

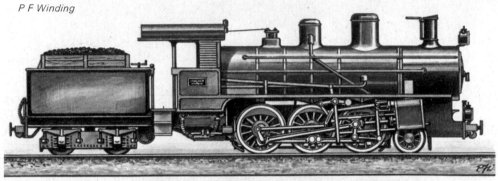

High-Adhesion Locomotives

THE ENGERTH-TYPE locomotive achieved prominence as a result of the Semmering trails, held in Austria in 1851 to ascertain the best type of adhesion locomotive for working steep gradients. The original concept was what would now be regarded as an 0-6-4T, except that the two rear axles were mounted in a frame distinct from the main frame, and attached thereto by a pivot located behind the driving wheels. Thus the whole of the rear frame could move radially, while at the same time a proportion of its weight could be transferred to the main frame through the bearing pivot by a suitable adjustment of the springs, thereby increasing the total weight on the driving wheels available for adhesion.

In some of the earliest designs, there was a rear coupling between the driving and trailing wheels so that the rear part of the engine was also driven; later on, the practice was found to be unsound and was abandoned. Another common fault with some designs was that the

weight transference was often more imaginary than real, and many were converted to tender engines. Even so, the Engerth type enjoyed a wide popularity in Europe, and at least two examples have been preserved.

Our illustrations depict the final development of this type of locomotive as supplied to several metre-gauge railways in the north of Spain by the firm of J A Maffei, from 1913 onwards. The lines concerned abound in sharp curves and steep gradients which require locomotives with a maximum adhesive weight and considerable flexibility.

The Maffei engines were extremely successful under those conditions because as well as the radial freedom of the tender mainframe about the support pivot, the tender bogie was also arranged to turn on its central pivot. In addition, the leading end of the locomotive was carried on a Krauss-Melmholtz truck to actuate the intermediate coupled wheels, thus reducing the rigid wheelbase to 9ft 2in. The spring suspension was also far more sophisticated than in the earlier designs, and included compensation for the relative roll between the two main frames.

In Germany, where similar designs have been widely employed on narrow-gauge railways, the Engerth layout is known as a supporting tender (Stutz-tender) locomotive.

TRAINS IN THE MOUNTAINS

Mountain Railways of Switzerland

A RhB Class G4/5 2-8-0 locomotive with an excursion train in May 1967 on the Rhatische Bahn (Rhaetian Railway) pictured near Klosters, Switzerland. The Rhaetian is the largest private metre-gauge railway in Switzerland and is in the largest Canton, Graubunden. The first Rhaetian railway line which opened in the summer of 1890 was an 8-mile narrow-gauge track from Landquart through Klosters to Davos. Six years after its opening, the line was extended to Chur and then as far as Thusis. In 1904 the Rhaetian line reached St Moritz and thereafter branches were opened between Reichenau and Ilaz, between Sameden and Pontresina, and between Davos and Filisur. In 1912 and 1913, further branch lines were opened up between Lanz and Disentis, and between Bever and Schuls-Tarasp. The Bernina Railway, a 37-mile line from Tirano to San Moritz built between 1908 and 1910, was absorbed in 1943.

When the system eventually changed from steam to electric traction, some of the steam locomotives were retained for works trains. Today the system is entirely electrically operated, apart from occasional excursions as illustrated overleaf. The seven most-recently acquired locomotives of the Rhatische Bahn are 2,400hp units with Bo-Bo-Bo wheel arrangement designed easily to adapt to the sharpest curves and to be capable of pulling trains of up to 265 tonnes (260 tons); a typical train would consist of anything up to 13 bogie coaches. The locomotives are named after the main towns on the system. The line also possess 10 Bo-BO 1,600hp engines, and some earlier C-Cs with centre cabs and some 1-D-1 locomotives. Rolling stock consists of spacious and comfortable bogie corridor coaches which, on the principal trains, are accompanied by a restaurant car.

The Rhatische Bahn operates a total of 244 route-miles and on account of its mountain location, provides some of the most breathtaking scenery in the country. One main section of the system is that linking Chur to Filisur via Landquart, Klosters and Davos. From Landquart the line enters a tunnel to emerge in the Pratigau valley from which the resort town of Klosters is reached. A tunnel now permits through running where in previous years there was a terminal station. A 1 in 20 incline, the steepest gradient on any Rhaetian main line, is encountered on leaving Klosters whence it passes through the modern station at the internationally famous ski centre of Davos.

Right: Car on the Beckenried-Klewenalp cable railway above Lake Lucerne. *J Winkley*

Facing page: A car on the rack-and -pinion Pilatus Railway in Switzerland, opened in 1889. It is the world's steepest railway, climbing over 5,300ft in just over 2½ miles from the shore of Lake Lucerne to the Pilatus summit. *J L Champion*

Picture overleaf: *B Stephenson*

Rhatische Bahn 2-8-0 and train near Klosters, Switzerland.

Above: Preserved steam locomotives heading a special train on the Rhaetian line. *D R Stopher*

Left: Two of the Pilatus rack railway's cars at the Alpnachstad terminus in May 1967. *B Stephenson*

Below left: A Rigi Railway motor coach with lowered pantograph coasts over Schnurtobel bridge with a Rigi Kulm-Vitznau train. *B Stephenson*

Below: Brienz-Rothorn Railway 0-4-2T rack locomotive approaching Planalp with a train descending from Rothorn Kulm to Brienz. *Mrs M Stephenson*

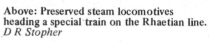

Above, left and left below: Three views of one of two veteran steam locomotives of the Vitznau-Rigi Railway, No 17, at the lakeside station and on the climb of the Rigi. Although the line is now electrified, the steam engines are still used for special excursions.
all G M Kichenside

Below: A 1952 electric railcar on the Gornergrat Railway in August 1971.
W H R Godwin

Top: Water stop at Planalp halfway up the Brienzer-Rothorn Railway, last all-steam line in Switzerland. *M Gower*

Left: Train on the Arth-Rigi Railway on the final mile to the summit above Staffel, with the Vitznau-Rigi track alongside. *D R Stopher*

Bottom right:.A cable car on the two-section line from Trubsee, above Engelberg, to the 10,000ft ridge near the summit of Titlis in a perpetual world of snow and ice. *G M Kichenside*

Top right: Electric locomotive of the Rhaetian Railway descending from Bergun with a St Moritz-Chur train in May 1967. *B Stephenson*

Railways on the Roof of the World

A READER WHO is not well-informed in railway matters might well receive with incredulity the information that there is a railway which climbs to a greater height than the summit of Mont Blanc, on standard gauge — not narrow gauge, and without any aid from rack-and-pinion traction; and, moreover, that this 15,848ft summit is but one of a number in the same region that top the 14,000ft mark after arduous climbs from their lower terminals at sea level. The region is South America; the countries concerned are Peru, Chile and Bolivia. and the reason for these airy exercises in railway engineering is the towering mountain mass of the Andes, which borders the Pacific coast of South America throughout its entire length.

In the heart of the Andes is considerable mineral wealth, of nitrate, copper and silver, and whereas the coastal side of the mountains is in large measure completely barren, there are high-lying valleys near the equator in which the temperate climate encourages sheep farming and agricultural activity also. It is to connect these sources of revenue with the coast that railways such as the Peruvian Central, the Peruvian Southern, the Antofagasta (Chile) & Bolivia and the Argentine Transandine, to name the most important, have been carried up into the forbidding mountain range.

By far the most difficult of the Transandean lines to operate is the one that reaches the maximum altitude of 15,848ft, the Central Railway of Peru. It owes its planning and construction to an American adventurer named Henry Meiggs, so much so indeed that at the close of last century it was widely known as the Meiggs road in Peru. What he conceived orginally was a Central Transandine Railway, which ultimately came into existence as the Callao, Lima & Lima & Oroya Railway, but in 1890 became the Central of Peru Division of the Peruvian Corporation Railways. So it is from Callao, the chief Pacific port of Chile, that this remarkable railway starts its 216-mile course towards the interior. From there it is a run of a few miles only to the Peruvian capital, Lima, where, in the Desamparados station, the journey of the two daily trains to Oruro really begins. One, of lightweight stock, is the *Rapido*. The other, which follows, is heavier and slower, and does the roadside work.

From Lima the line makes straight for the great mountain chain of the Andes, the Cordillera. At first the rise up the Rimac valley, to Chosica, is gradual; in the first 25 miles the average gradient is a little easier than 1 in 100, but climbing then begins in earnest. The ruling gradient steepens officially to 1 in 25, and enginemen at least have little doubt that up some pitches 1 in 20 is nearer the mark. The steeper climb is continuous for 73 miles, until at the Galera tunnel the line crosses the Continental Divide at an altitude of 15,848ft.

On the grounds of expense spiral tunnelling to gain height was ruled out; instead, the line climbs up

precipitous mountain slopes by an endless succession of zig-zags, or V-switches, each of which requires reversal of the train at the two ends, greatly increasing the journey time. Most of the climbing is up deep mountain valleys which are completely barren, though the line runs through a few towns, such as Matucana, and several smelting plants. Of tunnels there are plenty, and great viaducts over gorges joining the main valley.

Also plentiful in such country are hazards to trains, particularly from boulders breaking loose from the mountain-sides and falling on to the railway. Trolleys manned by two men, called pilot gravity cars, are run regularly down the grades ahead of the passenger trains

Top: A modern diesel railcar and a German-built steam locomotive side-by-side on the Southern line near Cuzco in 1969.
C & D Gannon

Above left: Puenta Ruinas station deep in the Urubamba canyon, near Machu Picchu on the Southern Railway of Peru. C & D Gannon

Below left: Central railway station at Lima in 1970. D T Rowe

Below:
In the early days of the Central of Peru Railway, locomotive No 13 'Santa Domingo' heading a works train across Verrugas bridge. Ian Allan Library

to discover and warn if such rock-falls have taken place. For the relief of passengers who might suffer from mountain sickness at the great altitude reached on the climb cylinders of oxygen are carried in the trains.

Before entering the 1,287yd Galera tunnel the train stops at Ticlio, which at 15,610ft above the sea is the highest railway junction in the world — "cold, dismal and lonesome", as one account has it. The junction is for the original Marococha loop, which reaches the record altitude of 15,848ft; the Galera tunnel was bored in later years to provide a shorter and slightly easier route eastwards. Curiously enough, even at this tremendous altitude snow gives little trouble to the operating staff;

the reason, of course, is the nearness of the Equator, as a result of which the snowline is as high as 17,000ft. The run from the Galera tunnel down to Oroya brings the level of the railway to 12,220ft, and there giant smelters proclaim one of the principal reasons for the railway's construction.

Oroya is the junction for the independent Cerro de Pasco Railway, which runs for 120 miles northwards along the Cordillera, at no point less than 12,722ft above sea level and, at its maximum (Alcococha), reaching 14,385ft; this line was laid to tap the great Cerro de Pasco copper deposits and other minerals. Meanwhile, the Central of Peru main line continues for 78 miles from Oroya down the Mantaro Valley, finishing at Huancayo, at 10,700ft, in a fertile valley that contrasts totally with the barren mountain gorges through which it has passed to that point. The Peruvian Government owns a metre gauge line that continues from Huancayo to Huancavelica.

In the southern part of the country there is the Southern Railway of Peru, another property of the Peruvian Corporation. Its starting point is at Mollendo, on the Pacific coast, and like the Peruvian Central it climbs into the interior on the standard 4ft 8½in gauge. The coastal strip there is wider and the climbing, though steep, is less abrupt and zigzag layout was unnecessary. The Peruvian Southern is very up-to-date in its equipment and diesel-electric locomotives are the mainstay of its tractive power.

At La Joya, 55 miles from Mollendo, where the line has climbed to 4,441ft, it is joined by a 39-mile branch from the port of Matarani, which was opened in 1952. Matarani, north of Mollendo, is the safer and better-equipped harbour of the two, and now handles the bulk of the railway's freight traffic. Climbing continues as far as Arequipa, the most important town on the route and the railway's headquarters. Apart from one or two ravines, the line is entirely out in the open in rolling upland country — differing totally from the fearsome gorges threaded by the Peruvian Central — with views for many miles of the graceful snowclad cone of the 19,163ft Mount Misti, an extinct volcano.

At last, 233 miles from the coast, the summit level is reached at Crucero Alto, 14,608ft up. About 72 miles further on is Juliaca, at 12,551ft altitude, a junction from which the line to Cuzco bears away for 210 miles to the north-west, through some of the finest sheep-rearing country in Peru, and finishes in what was formerly the capital of the Inca empire, with its notable megalithic remains. Still more interesting is the continuation of the main line from Juliaca to Puno, at the north-western end of the most astonishing lake in the world, Titicaca, 130 miles long and up to 41 miles wide, at an altitude of 2,466ft.

At Puno the *Peruvian* Southern takes to the water, on which it maintains a fleet of five ships. The most interesting of them is the SS *Inca,* which was built at Hull, sailed across the Atlantic, round Cape Horn and up the Pacific coast to Mollendo; there the ship was taken to pieces for transit up the railway to Puno, where it was put together again and finally launched on Titicaca. This ship and the SS *Ollanta* (also built at Hull) both have sleeping accommodation for the overnight journey along the length of the lake, which takes 12 hours.

The lake voyage ends on Bolivian soil, at Guaqui, the terminus of a 60-mile metre-gauge line which links Lake Titicaca with the Bolivian capital, La Paz, and which by

Top: Bolivian 2-8-4T No 553 in bright new paint at Oruro in 1970. *D T Rowe*

Centre: A diesel railcar at Cochabamba station in 1970. *D T Rowe*

Right: A 2-8-2 locomotive heads a freight at Cochabamba on Bolivian National Railways, with which Southern of Peru steamer services on Lake Titicaca connect. *D T Rowe*

are operated by rack-and-pinion on a 1 in 6 gradient has always limited its usefulness.

The other line coming into Viacha is (or was, for reasons to be described in a moment) the Antofagasta (Chile) & Bolivia, from the Pacific port of Antofagasta, 701 miles to the south. All three metre-gauge lines combine to use the 18½-mile stretch of the Guaqui-La Paz line from Viacha to the Bolivian capital, passing at El Alto, 13,396ft, over the rim of the great basin in which lies La Paz, Down its precipitous side is the 5½-mile drop of 1,370ft, negotiated with electric power on a gradient which at its steepest is 1 in 14½. It was brought into use in 1905 and was the first railway electrification in South America.

The Antofagasta (Chile) & Bolivia Railway, or FCAB, is by far the biggest of the independent Andean lines and formerly had a total route mileage of 1,821. Immediately after the Pacific War of 1879-1882 between Bolivia and Chile had cut Bolivia off from the Pacific coast and pushed the frontier back inland for several hundred miles, a beginning was made with a line on the very narrow gauge of 2ft 6in from the port of Antofagasta north-eastwards, to tap the nitrate deposits. After the war the Chilian Government authorised the railway to extend to the new frontier at Ollague, 274 miles from Antofagasta, passing on its way over a summit level of 12,976ft at Ascotan. A 60-mile branch was thrown off northwards from Ollague to Collahuassi, the centre of an extremely rich copper-mining region, which at Punto Alto reached the world's second highest railway altitude of 15,835ft; this section of the branch has now been abandoned.

Before Ascotan summit the railway enters a stretch of line which for 500 miles continuously is never below the 12,000ft level. In 1889 a Bolivian mining company had extended the line, but on the metre gauge, for 110 miles from Ollague to Uyuni, and in that year a British company not only took over the Antofagasta-Ollague line, but also, by consent of the Bolivian Government, the Uyuni extension, adding further to the latter by 101 miles to reach the important mining centre of Oruro by 1892.

Then in 1903 the Bolivia Railway Company was formed to lay 126 miles of line from Oruro to the junction at Viacha already mentioned, together with two very important branches, one of 132 miles from Oruro to Cochabamba, and the other of 109 miles from Rio Mulato to Potosi. The latter is distinguished by possessing the highest railway station in the world — Condor, 15,705ft above the sea — and also for tapping what to date has been the world's greatest deposit of silver, a mountain at Potosi which is calculated to have produced about £350 million-worth of the precious metal!

In 1903 the FCAB took over the working of the main line from Uyuni to Viacha. For many years all went well, except for the troublesome change of gauge from 2ft 6in to one metre at Uyuni which meant transhipment of both passengers and freight. At last the courageous decision was reached to widen the narrower gauge — an immense task, involving 236 miles of track. Before the major operation took place, 56 miles had been converted to mixed gauge by laying a third rail; then, after meticulous preparation like that of the Great Western Railway of England in changing its principal main lines in the 1890s from 7ft to 4ft 8½in gauge, in 1928 the FCAB carried out 180 miles of track widening

agreement with the Bolivian Government is operated by the Peruvian Southern. About 40 miles out from Guaqui the line reaches Viacha, an unpretentious station which nevertheless is a junction of some note. There it joins the Arica-La Paz Railway, which comes up from the Pacific coast over a 13,963ft summit at Jeneral Lagos, to provide by far the shortest route (293 miles) between La Paz and the sea. However, poor port facilities at Arica and the fact that 26 miles of the climb up from the coast

Above: One of the Alco Co-Co 2,150hp diesel-electric locomotives developed for high-altitude work on the Peru Southern line in 1961. *Alco Products Inc*

Left: A Bolivian 2-8-2 heads a freight at Cochabamba in 1970. *D T Rowe*

Below left: A Garratt steam locomotive of the Antofagasta line at La Paz-Alta, Bolivia. *P B Whitehouse*

Bottom: Bolivian National Japanese-built 1,870hp Bo-Bo-Bo diesel-electric locomotive at Oruro in 1970. *D T Rowe*

in only six days, fortunately in fine weather — a remarkable feat at over 12,000ft altitude.

After the widening was completed, the FCAB International Limited at last began to run through from Antofagasta to La Paz, with the journey time cut from 42 to 31 hours. For a long time powerful 2-8-4 steam tank locomotives worked the principal trains, but in more recent years the inevitable diesel-electrics began to make their appearance.

In its efficient management and operation the FCAB has always had a high reputation, but the picture has now changed. Traffic has been lost through the opening of new roads parallel to the railway, and passenger traffic also has been lost to air competition. But the worst trouble has been with the Bolivian Government, notorious for its instability, which by degrees imposed such onerous conditions on the railway that in February 1959 the FCAB entirely suspended its operation in Bolivia, save only over the main line between Ollague and Oruro. While the Chilean section of the FCAB is still efficiently run, the Bolivian lines have gone into a sad decline.

Of many other railways in the Andes, most of them relatively small privately owned concerns, one other, very much farther to the south, deserves mention. It is the 155-mile Transandine Railway proper, which is partly in the Argentine Republic and partly in Chile and has had a chequered history. It was first planned in 1889 but owing to many delays it was not until 1910 that the two sections met in the 3,464yd-long Cumbre tunnel (the summit) at 10,452ft above sea level. At its eastern end the Transandine linked up at the city of Mendoza with the former Buenos Aires & Pacific Railway (now the Ferrocarril General San Martin), and at its western end, at Los Andes, with the Chilean State Railways, both of 5ft 6in gauge, although the Transandine itself has always been of metre gauge. From Mendoza the gradients up the gorge of the Mendoza river at first are not more severe than 1 in 40, but nearing the summit tunnel the inclination steepens to 1 in 16, with rack-and-pinion traction. On the Chilean side the descent is considerably more abrupt, with a fall of 7,750ft in 44 miles, and the rack-and-pinion sections steepen to 1 in 12. This handicap led to the electrification of the Chilean section in 1923.

In its heyday the Transandine did well, even to the extent of operating a daily Pullman train between Mendoza and Los Andes. The train took 12 hours to complete the journey of 155 miles, and it formed the link in a 38½-hour rail journey between Buenos Aires and Santiago. Being well south of the Equator, snow caused considerable operating difficulties in winter, but Nature could impose far worse hazards than mere snowfall. In January 1934, in one of the lateral valleys feeding the Mendoza river a large lake formed high up in the mountains due to the formation of a massive dam of ice. When the ice wall gave way a vast mass of water swept down into the Mendoza valley, completely obliterating many miles of the railway.

Ten years elapsed before sufficient finance became available to restore the track, but by then conditions had changed; the railway had to face air competition and soon afterwards that of a new motor road over the Cumbres pass. As a consequence, the Transandine Railway today, the two halves of which have been taken over by the national systems of Argentine and Chile, is steadily losing its former importance.

An Austrian Rack Railway

THE FOLLOWING PICTURE CAPTURES some of the colour and the character of Austria's only Riggenbach rack line, the Achenseebahn. The line runs from the peaceful town of Jenbach in the valley of the River Inn to Achensee about four miles to the north.

Built in 1888, this picturesque steam railway with its quaint locomotives, constructed in the same year at the Floridsdorf works in Vienna, and which look as if they might have been designed by Emmett, is unusual in more than one respect. Being a rack and adhesion line, the cylinders are placed horizontally and the piston rods drive small wheels each side which are positioned between the two axles and about 10in above the rails. To enable the locomotives to run on either rack or plain track, the wheels drive a shaft which connects with both a central rack cog and the four driving wheels by means of gears and connecting rods. The transmission system accounts for the distinctly odd appearance of the wheels which take the drive from the cylinders revolving in the opposite direction to that in which the locomotive is travelling.

The Riggenbach rack differs from the Abt system in that it is composed of a 3in deep and 4in wide channel, spanned by close-fitting rungs on which the rack wheel engages.

A typical train on the Achenseebahn would consist of one of the four locomotives pushing or pulling one or two green four-wheeled coaches. From the station at Jenbach the line runs east past its own sheds before engaging the rack to negotiate first a 1 in 10 gradient then a little further on a 1 in 5. The rack ends at Eben, 28 mintues' run from the terminus at Jenbach, the line emerging from a forest to form a loop beside a hotel.

Here the adhesion system is brought into effect and the locomotive is uncoupled, run round the coaches and connected at the front for the level run to the next stop, the village of Maurach. After a brief wait, the train resumes its journey and crosses the valley to arrive about five minutes later at Seespitz. The road and railway line run side by side until the track ends at the wooden station of Achensee to connect with a ferry service on the lake.

Few structures decorate the Achensee-bahn apart from the shed and works mentioned earlier and an impressive timber station at Achensee. Owing to a shortage of space at the upper terminal, there are no turnouts or loops; all works and service track face on to a hand-operated traverser giving simple, if rather laborious, transfer of stock from one track to another.

Picture overleaf: *J L Champion*

53

Achenseebahn train at the top of the rack.

LAST DAYS OF STEAM IN PICTURES

Steam virtually disappeared from the railways of North America during the 1950's and most of Europe has now followed suit. There is still one (and one only) large American road to operate steam, the Denver & Rio Grande Western, who run their 3 ' 0" gauge branch from Durango to Silverton as a tourist attraction. Elsewhere any steam operations are in private hands, mainly as tourist railroads.

In Europe too, the changeover has come quickly and Britain's nationalised railway system has but one steam operated line – like the Denver & Rio Grande's it is narrow gauge, though this time the gauge is 2 ' 0". Again it is a summer only service, it runs from Aberystwyth to Devil's Bridge.

On the mainland of Europe steam still lingers on, mainly in Germany and the Eastern Bloc, though at the time of writing France still steams the odd American-built 1-4-1R and Italy has scattered outposts in regular operation. Spain, once a steam stronghold, has little, and Portugal only on those lines around Porto and on the narrow gauge.

To see big steam in action one must now go to Africa and Asia, and even here it is on the wane, though the current world shortage of oil may retard the changeover. In Asia it is in India and Pakistan that steam is still in the ascendancy and likely to remain so for some time yet. Southern Africa and Portuguese West and East Africa are still strongholds, and the East African countries of Kenya, Uganda and Tanzania retain their huge red Garratts. But time is running out and in a few years it will all be a memory.

In the far South and East, Australia has little steam bar some preserved locomotives and the same applies to New Zealand, Japan, in the North can be steamy, but as with other parts of the world this will not last long either.

America–The Final Years

Above: Norfolk & Western Railway streamlined K2 4-8-2 No 132 at Roanoke, Va, in September 1951. *J M Jarvis*

Left: Norfolk & Western Railway Mallet No 2174 on Trace Fork Viaduct, in the Allegheny mountains, in November 1959. *D K Johnson*

Left: On CP in 1959, Pacific No 2470 leaving Montreal Windsor Street station. *J N Westwood*

Bottom: Milwaukee Road Pacific No 165 leaving Chicago with a local train in Summer 1952. *J M Jarvis*

Right: Norfolk & Western Class J 4-8-4 on a southbound train in the scenic New River gorge at Pembroke, Virginia, in September 1951. *J M Jarvis*

Some British Mainliners

Below: Bridge of the Clyde Valley line near Crawford with BR standard Class 5-hauled northbound goods train in March 1964.
D Cross

Bulleid Southern Railway Battle of Britain
Pacific No 34051 'Winston Churchill'
M Chapman

Above: One of the powerful King-class 4-6-0s in action on the GW Birmingham line, passing North Acton. *M Pope*

Left: Memorial mural to the founder engineer of the Great Western, adjacent to the remains of Birmingham Snow Hill station. *J R Batts*

63

A Class 8F 2-8-0 with a freight train crossing the West Coast main line at Wigan in December 1965. *M J Esau*

LMS Class 5 4-6-0 No 44680 heading a Stephenson Locomotive Society special train at Wrexham in 1967. This was the last steam train out of Birmingham (Snow Hill) *J Adams*

A BR Class 8F climbing away from Chinley to Chapel-en-le-Frith in February 1968. *D Huntriss*

SIR NIGEL GRESLEY

N° 4498
A 4   KINGS +

Narrow Gauge and Industrial

Above: British Rail's only steam line: Vale of Rheidol locomotive No 9 'Prince of Wales' *British Rail*

Left: Robert Stephenson & Hawthorns 1940 0-4-0CT 'Roker' at work at Doxford's shipyard, Sunderland, in April 1968. *Colourviews*

Facing page: LNER No 4498 'Sir Nigel Gresley' as restored to original condition minus valences. *B A Reeves*

Steam in Europe

CZECH RAILWAYS
Right: Czechoslovak pas de deux between a 2-6-2 and a Pacific on the bridge at Prague in October 1967. *C J Gammell*

FRENCH RAILWAYS
Below left: SNCF Class 231D Pacific on a Le Havre-Paris express in May 1966. *J B Snell*

Centre right: A class 230D 4-6-0 at Etaples *Colourviews*

Bottom right: 141TC 2-8-2 tank locomotives on push-and-pull trains at Paris Gare du Nord. *C M Whitehouse*

GERMAN STATE RAILWAYS

Above: Class 03 Pacific No 03 244 leaving Cochem, Moselle valley, with a Saarbrucken-Cologne express in August 1964. *B Stephenson*

Facing page: German Federal Railway Class O52 2-10-0 on an Eutingen-Horb train in May 1971. *R Bastin*

**PORTUGUESE STATE
RAILWAYS**

Portuguese National Railways 4-6-0
No 294 crossing Tua bridge with a
Porto-Barca d'Alva train in
September 1971. *A G Orchard*

Facing page: Portuguese 1886
Kessler-built 2-6-0T No E86
heading a train for Povoa into
Lousado station in 1972. *M Pope*

YUGOSLAV RAILWAYS

**Above: Yugoslav Railways Class 83
engine shunting at Dubrovnik in
September 1969.** *R A H Casling*

Where Steam Still Rules

INDIAN GOVERNMENT RAILWAYS

Top: A full load for B-class 0-4-0ST No 788 locomotive and coaches at Jalpaiguri on the roadside track of the Darjeeling Himalayan light railway. *L G Marshall*

Centre: Class WP Pacific No 7434 ready for a turn at Agra in February 1968. *E Talbot*

Bottom: At the other end of the scale, No 32 of the 2ft-gauge Howrah Amta (Light) Railway taking water at a wayside station. *E Talbot*

EAST AFRICAN RAILWAYS

EAR 4-8-0 No 2412 on the shore of Lake Victoria at Kisumu, Kenya, with a Butere train in January 1971. *C J Gammell*

RAILWAYS OF SOUTH AFRICA

Above: SAR Class 24 NBL 4-8-4 at De Aar in October 1971. *D T Rowe*

Right: South African GEA-class Beyer-Garratt 4-8-2 + 2-8-4 with a train of empty fruit wagons in April 1971. *T B Owen*

WEST AFRICA
Benguela Railway's Beyer-Garratt No N340
at Caimbambo Station in Angola in 1968.
Conway Picture Library

Scenic run on the preserved Silverton tourist railway in Colorado in August 1966. *C J Gammell*

RAILS ACROSS THE ROCKIES

OVER A DISTANCE of something like 1,500 miles, from Canada through the United States down to Mexico, there runs the great mountain rampart of the Rockies. It forms what is known as the Continental Divide, between the watersheds of rivers running eastwards and southwards to the Atlantic, and of those with considerably shorter courses westwards to the Pacific. In certain areas the Divide is a long way away from the Pacific coast — near Denver, Colorado, for example, not far short of 1,000 miles — but the space between the main ranges and the coast is filled almost entirely with mountainous country, so that most of the railways which make their way through from the Middle West to the Pacific have to negotiate at least two if not three summits en route.

The west coast of South America similarly is bordered by the great range of the Andes, which are even higher than the Rockies and with a much narrower strip of country between mountains and sea. The railways of Peru and Chile have been engineered up to almost incredible heights — over 15,000ft above the sea in some cases — in search of the mineral and agricultural wealth of the interior and to bring those products down to the coast for shipment. But the railways which have penetrated the Rockies have done so for a different reason — to link the great cities of Washington, Oregon and California (Seattle, Tacoma, Portland, San Francisco, Los Angeles and so on) with the Middle West and the Eastern states of the USA. Indeed, just as the Canadian Pacific Railway was the price demanded by Columbia (now British Columbia) for adhesion to the Canadian Confederation, so in the 1840s Oregon might have opted to become an independent republic had not steps been taken to provide rail communication between that territory and the rapidly growing United States of

America.

Even so, it was not until 1853 that the USA Congress passed an Act directing the Secretary of War to establish the Pacific Railroad Surveys to determine the most feasible railway routes from the Mississippi basin to the Pacific. Jefferson Davis was the Secretary at that time, and although he was not entirely impartial, favouring possible routes more to the south than to the north (on the ground that operation of the latter in winter would be more difficult), his survey parties were given a fairly free hand. Their work was monumental in extent, covering meteorological and many other factors as well as practicable routes.

Two of the recommendations of the survey report, published in 1855, was that on any chosen route the gradients should not exceed in steepness the 2.2 per cent, or 1 in 45, which had been found reasonably workable on the Baltimore & Ohio Railroad in the east; and that the curves should not be sharper than those common on that main line. As in Canada, however, progress with construction was slow and it took until 1869 to link Union Pacific and Central Pacific tracks at Promontory summit, just north of the Great Salt Lake in Utah, to complete the first trans-continental railway in the United States. After that progress was much more rapid, and a number of routes which had been recommended by the Pacific Railroad Surveys soon were being threaded by railway tracks. Space forbids any attempt to give a history of each project, but it is worth while to describe the outstanding features of each route.

Nearest of the lines to the 49th Parallel (the border with Canada) was the Great Northern which started from the twin cities of St Paul and Minneapolis in the Middle West and extended for 1,454 miles to Spokane, from which a line owned jointly with the Northern Pacific Rly (the Spokane, Portland & Seattle) brought portions of its trans-continental trains into the city of Portland, Oregon. The main trains, of which the most important was the Empire Builder, continued to Seattle, 1,784 miles from St Paul, and to Tacoma, 40 miles farther on. The GNR, after many miles of easy grade across the prairies, got across the Continental Divide through the Marias pass, at 5,231ft altitude, with approach grades up to 1 in 100 westbound and 1 in 55 eastbound; by a steeper obstacle was near the end of the journey, between Spokane and Seattle, where the 2,818ft summit of the Stevens pass was finally conquered by boring the 7.79-mile Cascade tunnel, the longest bore in the United States. The route of the Empire Builder extended in the east as far as Chicago and was handled between Chicago and St Paul by the Chicago, Burlington & Quincy RR.

Built to the south of the Great Northern was the Northern Pacific, also starting from St Paul and Minneapolis, but pursuing a more southerly route through Billings and Butte to Spokane, 1,496 miles of the Great Northern. Through coaches on Trains to and from Portland were worked, as were those of the GNR, by the Spokane, Portland & Seattle Rly. The NPR main line continued from Spokane to a junction called East Auburn, where its trains split into two for Tacoma and Seattle; Tacoma was 1,889 miles from St Paul and Seattle three miles more. In crossing the Continental Divide the Northern Pacific had to negotiate two summits just about 100 miles apart at the Homestake Pass, 6,328ft, and the Mullan Pass, 5,566ft. Shortly before Seattle, also like the Great Northern, the Northern Pacific reached the Cascade range, but got over it at 2,822ft altitude in the Stampede tunnel. The principal NPR express was the North Coast Limited, which was hauled by the Burlington line between Chicago and St Paul.

Class F45 EMD 3,600hp diesel-electric locomotive with GM 20-cylinder engine.

A full dome car used on BN top passenger services.

Class E8A EMD 2,250hp diesel-electric locomotive used on Chicago commuter service.

Class SW1500 EMD 1,500hp diesel-electric shunter.

Clifford & Wendy Meadway

100-ton coal hopper of 1970 delivery.

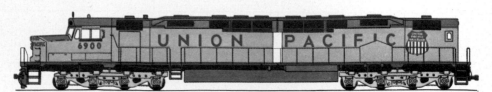

Union Pacific Centennial diesel-electric
locomotive Class DDA 40X of 6,600hp.

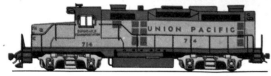

Class GP20 general-purpose 2,000hp
diesel-electric switcher.

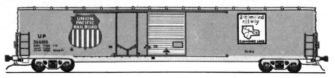

UP standard boxcars range from 50ft to 86ft
in length and have hydraulically
cushioned underframes.

UP Pullman as used in remaining
long-distance passenger services.

Open gondala wagon for 70-ton loads.

From March 1970 the Great Northern Railway and Northern Pacific Railway, which jointly owned the Chicago, Burlington & Quincy Railroad and the Spokane, Portland & Seattle Railway, were merged, to form Burlington Northern Inc.

Next to the south comes the Chicago, Milwaukee, St Paul & Pacific Railroad, one of two companies to possess a main line right through from Chicago to the Pacific coast, extending for 2,189 miles to Seattle and 2,227 miles to Tacoma. Between 1915 and 1927 the Milwaukee road tackled the tremendous task of electrifying 665 miles of that main line, through the most difficult sections — 438 miles from Harlowton to Avery, over the Loweth and Pipestone Pass summits (5,804 and 6,352ft respectively), and for 227 miles through the Cascade range, over the Snoqualmie pass. The Milwaukee was fairly late in the field with a 'show' transcontinental train, but in the summer of 1947 there was added to the distinguished family of Milwaukee Hiawathas the Olympian Hiawatha, on a 45-hour schedule between Chicago and Seattle, with all the latest in luxury equipment. It was destined like so many other famous American trains, to have but a short life, in this case of 14 years only.

With little doubt, the most important of all the main lines linking the Middle West with the Pacific Coast is the Union Pacific. first of the rails across the Rockies to be completed, in 1869, the UP did not get nearer to Chicago than Omaha; for many years its through expresses were handled to and from that Middle-West centre over 488 miles of the Chicago & North Western line, but in 1955 the traffic was handed over to the progressive Chicago, Milwaukee, St Paul & Pacific, whose route was of exactly the same length.

Over nearly the whole 990 miles of the main line from Omaha to Ogden, Utah, the UP has the unique distinction, for the USA, of double track throughout. At Julesburg, 363 miles from Omaha, a 197-mile branch diverges to the south-west to Denver, capital of Colorado; next, at Granger, 844 miles, a 944-mile line takes off north-west to Portland, Oregon; from Ogden another tentacle stretches south-westerly 821 miles across the desert country of Utah and Nevada finally to reach Los Angeles. A short section of the last-named line, across the Cajon pass from Barstow, is shared with the Atchison, Topeka & Santa Fe Railway. But what of San Francisco? Eventually the former Central Pacific RR, which in 1869 met the westward-advancing Union Pacific at Promontory, was absorbed by the Southern Pacific Railroad, and it is the SPRR that takes over at Ogden from the UPRR for the 785-mile run to San Francisco.

Another distinction of the Union Pacific is that of reaching the second highest altitude of all the transcontinental lines. Climbing gradually westward from Omaha, after Cheyenne it faces the 1 in 65 ascent of Sherman hill, which takes it to a summit 8,013ft above the sea. For the next 360 miles the line is never less than 6,270ft up and it climbs finally at Aspen summit, 7,230ft,

before dropping down to Ogden. For tackling these gradients, the Union Pacific has always been noted for its motive power. In the days of steam, development led finally to the giant 4-8-4s, 4-12-2s (a unique wheel formation for freight service), and 4-6-6-4 and 4-8-8-4 Challenger and Big Boy articulated types. With its 14-wheel tender, the Big Boy type weighed an incredible 540 tons — the heaviest steam locomotive in the world. In later years the UPRR achieved distinction in another way, by introducing a fleet of powerful gas-turbine-electric locomotives for working freight over the 176 miles between Green River, Wyoming, and Ogden,

SOUTHERN SP PACIFIC

TOFC wagon of 65 short tons capacity and two refrigerated semi-trailers of joint SP-Union Pacific fruit transport company.

High-capacity boxcar with cushioned suspension for delicate loads.

Vert-a-Pac boxcar designed to carry partly assembled motorcars stacked vertically inside.

Double-deck passenger car for commuter services in the San Francisco area.

EMD 3,600hp SD45T-2 diesel-electric freight locomotive.

Clifford & Wendy Meadway

including the negotiation of Aspen summit. Now, however, diesels are again in sole possession.

The flatter stretch of the main line, for 400 miles west from Omaha, was a speedway of considerable note. Over it in the 1950s and 1960s there ran a procession of streamlined trains -- the City of Los Angeles, City of San Francisco, City of Portland, City of Denver, Challenger and others, with many station-to-station runs timed at 70mph and some up to 75mph. From Chicago to San Francisco and Los Angeles the mountains were no bar to overall speeds of 57.9mph and 56.8mph over distances of 2,301 and 2,257 miles respectively; over the 1,049 miles between Chicago and Denver the City of Denver managed an average of 66.8mph.

One final word about the Southern Pacific section of the 'Overland' route to San Francisco. The original line skirted the north shore of the Great Salt Lake, west of Salt Lake City, and included steep gradients and sharp curvature. Eventually the Southern Pacific decided to cut straight across the lake, which it did by tipping rock and soil to provide 20 miles of embankments, and bridging the remainder by piling with thousands of long trees to form a trestle viaduct. The new line, 31½ miles in length and straight and level, cut 44½ miles from the original route.

Three railways were associated in the next crossing farther to the south of the Continental Divide, at the point where the mountain peaks are furthest away from the Pacific. They are, first, the Chicago, Burlington & Quincy from Chicago to Denver (1,034 miles); then the Denver and Rio Grande Western, at over 4,000ft altitude throughout its length of 570 miles from Denver to Salt Lake City; and the 919-mile Western Pacific from Salt Lake City to Oakland Pier, San Francisco. As far as Denver the Burlington main line, though reaching the mile-high capital of Colorado, climbs only gradually; but

the Rio Grande section is another matter. The original Rio Grande main line went south from Denver to Pueblo before it turned west through the Grand Canyon of the Arkansas river -- the Royal Gorge -- and then over the Tennessee pass at an altitude of 10,039ft, with approach gradients as steep as 1 in 33. But in 1928 a new route was opened due west from Denver, climbing for 50 miles, mostly on a 1 in 50 gradient, to the east portal of the 6¾-mile Moffat tunnel, and joining the original route at Dotsero. This cut the distance by 175 miles and reduced the journey time by 5½ hours. Farther west the Rio Grande also has its 7,440ft Soldier summit, approached from the east up a 1 in 41 ascent. Moffat tunnel is 9,239ft above sea level.

West of Salt Lake City the Western Pacific closely parallels the Southern Pacific line as far as Winnemucca, and then for 116 miles from Portola to Oroville descends the spectacular Father River canyon on an almost continuous 1 in 100 inclination. Indeed, throughout its Chicago-San Francisco journey the California Zephyr, though not the fastest of the old competing trains, attracted many travellers because of the scenic glories of its journey. Its fastest travel was over the Burlington main line, in company with the Burlington's other Zephyrs, with timings up to 75mph from start to stop.

Colorado, heart of the Rockies, has provided a scenic backdrop to many local rail routes, past and present. Best known is the Silverton, a 3ft-gauge branch of Denver & Rio Grande Western RR, which is still steam-powered and now carries over 100,000 passengers in the summer season. Until 1968 the Silverton branch was linked by an equally scenic line (latterly freight-only) running along the Colorado-New Mexico border for about 200 miles between Durango and a standard-gauge connection at Alamosa. The 64 miles between Chama and Antonito were revived in 1971 as

Top: Rio Grande Southern (formerly Florence & Cripple Creek) 4-6-0 No 20 preserved at the Colorado Railroad Museum. *V Goldberg*

Centre: Denver & Rio Grande California Zephyr, with dome car, at Helper, Utah, in June 1969. *V Goldberg*

Bottom: Historic link-up at Promontory in May 1869 between CP & UP *Union Pacific Railroad Museum*

the Cumbres & Toltec Scenic Railroad, jointly owned by the two states and worked by a contractor.

About 75 miles south of Denver, near Colorado springs, is one of only two rack railways in the US — the standard-gauge Manitou & Pike's Peak Railway which climbs to 14,109 feet in 8.9 miles. It is worked by old General Motors-powered stock and some more-recent Swiss-built diesel cars. Relics from the many vanished lines in the district have been rescued and are on display at the Colorado Railroad Museum at Golden, 10 miles west of Denver.

Finally, there is the Atchison, Topeka & Santa Fe Railway, which shares with the Milwaukee the distinction of owning through tracks from Chicago to the Pacific Coast — in the case of the Santa Fe to both Los Angeles and San Francisco. After double track for 669 miles from Chicago through Kansas City to Hutchinson, the Santa Fe faces the most difficult conditions of all the transcontinental routes, with four high summits in succession over the Continental and Arizona Divides. Raton pass comes first (7,573ft), with an approach in part as steep as 1 in 28; then Glorieta (7,437ft); Campbell pass (7,247ft); and Flagstaff (7,310ft). after which comes the tremendous drop to Needles, in the Colorado river valley, at 483ft altitude. But that is not all, for before the line reaches Los Angeles there is the Cajon pass to be tackled, with a 3,822ft summit.

In the heyday of the 1950s and 1960s a procession of distinguished trains used the Santa Fe main line daily — the all-Pullman extra-fare Super-Chief, the Chief, the El Capitan (conveying the equivalent of second-class passengers in reclining chairs, and made up latterly entirely of high-level cars), and the San Francisco Chief. Across the prairies very high speeds were run; all four trains mentioned were booked over the 127.2 miles from Gallup to Winslow in 102 minutes at 74.8mph, and there were other start-to-stop bookings exceeding 80mph. Over a line with such formidable gradients it was no mean achievement for the Super-Chief and the El Capitan both to cover the 2,226 miles between Chicago and Los Angeles in under 40 hours at an average speed of 56mph.

Today, although all the main lines described are carrying increasing freight traffic, because of air competition the passenger services have almost completely disappeared. Under the new National Railroad Passenger Corporation (Amtrak) there is still one combined Santa Fe super-Chief/El Capitan taking 40½ hours westbound and 40 hours eastbound for the Chicago-Los Angeles run. There is no longer a Burlington-Rio Grande-Western Pacific California Zephyr, though a Rio Grande Zephyr runs three times weekly between Denver and Salt Lake City. There is a daily Denver Zephyr between Chicago and Denver, continued three times a week to and from Cheyenne, and from there to San Francisco, replacing the former City of San Francisco.

To and from the North-west a daily Empire Builder still connects Chicago with Seattle, using Milwaukee tracks between Chicago and Minneapolis and the Great Northern line from there on; finally, three times a week a North Coast Limited runs between Chicago and Seattle via Minneapolis and the Northern Pacific line. All the present trains are composed of the best rolling stock acquired from the different railways, including dome, sleeping, chair and restaurant cars, but such a service is only a pale reflection of that which threaded the Rockies in the heyday of the American passenger train.

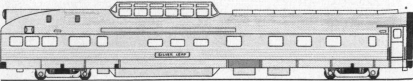

Denver & Rio Grande Western Railroad
dome car for Zephyr trains.

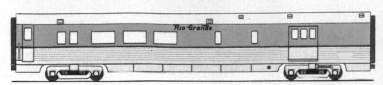

Baggage/crew car and diesel-electric locomotive for Zephyr trains.

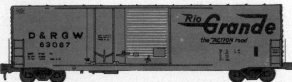

Class DE CC98 (EMD SD45) 3,600hp freight
locomotive.

Bogie boxcar of 75-ton load capacity.

Clifford & Wendy Meadway

Logo of the Atchison, Topeka &
Santa Fe Railway Company.

A container and a road semi-trailer on a
flat wagon designed for piggyback
traffic.

3,600hp diesel-electric locomotive as
used on 84-wagon coal trains.

Solid-bottom gondola car of the type
used on the 84-unit block coal trains.

Refrigerator wagon with mechanical
temperature control and shock-absorbing
underframe.

An EMD F45 diesel-electric locomotive
in earlier Santa Fe passenger colours,
now being repainted in the blue/yellow
livery seen above.

Clifford & Wendy Meadway

Top: Chicago & North Western Pacific No 1650 at Milwaukee in mid-1952. *J M Jarvis*

Left above: Union Pacific 4-8-4 at Cheyenne in September 1969. *P B Whitehouse*

Left: Denver & Rio Grande Western Railroad preserved 3ft gauge 2-8-2 engine and coaches on the Silverton, Colorado, tourist railway. *C J Gammell*

Below: Chicago, Milwaukee, St Paul & Pacific Railroad 4-6-2 No 885 on a local train out of Chicago in summer 1952. *J M Jarvis*

Facing page:
Above: Southern Pacific 0-6-0 switcher No 1268 at San Francisco in mid-1952. *J M Jarvis*

Below: Union Pacific 4-12-2 No 9032, a rare American three-cylinder engine, at Topeka, Kansas, in mid-1952. *J M Jarvis*

Above: Denver & Rio Grande Western class K36 2-8-2 No 488 climbs the 1 in 25 Cumbres pass with a special train in June 1964. *V Goldberg*

Right above: An original 1916 'Boxcab' electric locomotive of Milwaukee Road's Pacific Coast electrification at Tacoma, Washington State, in October 1970. *G G M Robinson*

Below: An electric locomotive– a 2-D-D-2 'Little Joe'–worked in multiple with three Geep diesels on the electrified section of the Milwaukee Road, with an eastbound freight at Deer Lodge, Montana, in October 1970. *G G M Robinson*

Right below: Atchison, Topeka & Santa Fe No 15 Texas Chief pictured at Oklahoma City before heading south. *C V Ehrke*

Rails in High Canada

Special 85ft coach with driving end for GO (Ontario) commuter trains, operated by Canadian National Railways.

Modern Canadian National stainless-steel passenger coach of Budd design with disc brakes.

CN Class GPA17 1,750hp diesel-electric locomotive.

CN Class GF30 3,000hp diesel-electric locomotive.

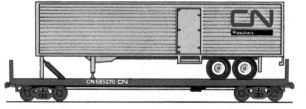

CN bogie flat wagon designed to take piggyback road semi-trailers up to 39ft 7in long.

OVERLEAF IS a four-unit diesel locomotive group heading the CP Rail Canadian train near the spectacular Great Divide in the Canadian Rockies, with Mount Cathedral's imposing peak in the background.

The Canadian Pacific Railway's main line is 3,363 miles in length and crosses the North American continent at its widest point, from Saint John, New Brunswick, to Vancover in British Columbia. The train named the Canadian, which is CPR's answer to the Canadian National Railway's Super Continental, runs from Montreal to Vancouver, taking nearly three days to complete the 2,880-mile journey.

For motive power in the days of steam, the Canadian was pulled by varying types of locomotive depending on the number of coaches (which at times amounted to as many as fifteen); in time Pacifics gave way to 4-8-2s and eventually to 4-6-4 Hudsons and a super-powerful type, the 2-10-4 weighing, with tender, nearly 330 tons. However, with the passing of steam and the advent of

diesels, two or three diesel-electric locomotives in multiple proved they could handle even the toughest parts of this mammoth journey with ease, as well as eliminating the former risk of forest fires sometimes started by steam engines in the past.

A very high standard of service is provided aboard the Canadian, which has accommodation comprising a scenic-dome lounge/sleeper complete with drawing-room and bedrooms, a scenic-dome coffee shop, stainless-steel sleepers with drawing-rooms, compartments and bedrooms, the last three being self-contained sleeping rooms. Roomettes, a smaller edition of the bedrooms, standard berths and reclining seats make up the rest of the overnight travel facilities.

Going west there are three time changes *en route*, at Thunder Bay, Swift Current and Field, so the full journey actually takes 71 hours 35 minutes. The eastbound trip, however, is one hour 10 minutes shorter. There are 37 regular stops with 30 conditional ones.

Profile of the lounge car shown at bottom left.

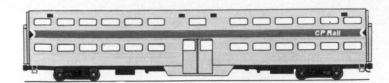

A 168-seat double-deck coach of a new commuter train introduced in 1970 by Canadian Pacific on its Montreal-Lake Shore service.

A 2400hp Bo-Bo diesel-electric locomotive of CP Rail Class DRF 24C built by M L Worthington in 1966.

A CP Rail 100-ton bottom-discharge covered hopper wagon.

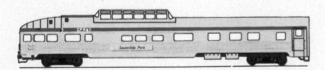

A CP Rail Park-class lounge car used in inter-city expresses such as the trans-continental Canadian.

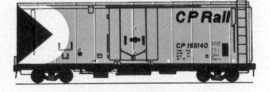

Standard insulated box car.

Picture overleaf: *CP Rail*

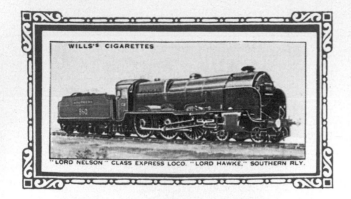

WILLS'S CIGARETTES

"LORD NELSON" CLASS EXPRESS LOCO. "LORD HAWKE," SOUTHERN RLY.

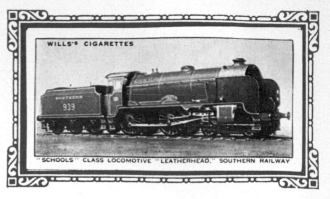

WILLS'S CIGARETTES

"SCHOOLS" CLASS LOCOMOTIVE "LEATHERHEAD," SOUTHERN RAILWAY

GEO. STEPHENSON'S R

WILLS'S CIGARETTES

EXPRESS LOCOMOTIVE "REMEMBRANCE," SOUTHERN RAILWAY

WILLS'S CIGARETTES

EXPRESS LOCOMOTIVE "KESTREL," GREAT NORTHERN RLY., IRELAND

HOBBIES AND MUSEUMS

Collecting Cigarette Cards

PRIOR TO WORLD WAR TWO each packed of British made cigarettes almost certainly contained a coloured card which formed one of a set of 50, covering popular interests. These could vary considerably in content, ranging from Footballers to Film Stars or Cars and Aeroplanes to Railway Engines. In most cases the manufacturers provided an album for a penny or twopence, and there was some competition among schoolboys to obtain the 'set' as quickly as possible. Today the cigarette card collecting hobby is comparatively rare, as are some of the issues of the cards themselves and sets in good condition can change hands at quite high figures. Not all cards however, end up in this type of collection for other specialist hobbies, that of railways for example, embrace these items as part of their love. Probably the two companies who chose railway subjects more often than others were Wills and Churchman though in later years Senior Service came up with some well produced photographic cards.

George Stephenson's 'Rocket' in its original
1829 form with inclined cylinders, as featured
in the Wills cigarette card series.

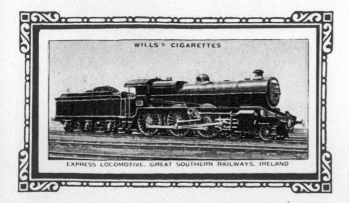

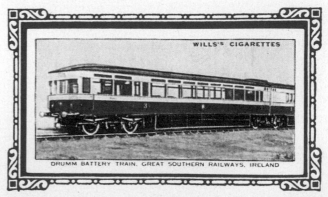

Railway Postage Stamps

JUST AS THE WAR with Napoleon went largely unnoticed in the novels of Jane Austen, so early railways were very sparsely represented on postage stamps, although social historians might regard them as equally significant. Europe did not notice railways until their centenaries, and one must go to Canada to find the first stamp issued specifically to celebrate the opening of a railway. That was the one-cent New Brunswick stamp of 1860, which had a locomotive design to mark the inauguration of the line from Pointe-au-Chene to Saint-Jean. Other values in the set, however, had different designs unconnected with the railway.

It was in 1860, also, that Peru took the decision to build a railway from the coast into the Andes to bring down the mineral wealth of zinc, lead, copper and silver mined around the town of Oroya. The coastal section of the line was the first railway in the country, and when it was opened in 1871 Peru issued a five-centavos stamp showing a 2-4-0 tender locomotive in profile within a border displaying the names of the principal places served (Callao, Lima and Chorrillos). The line was the genesis of the Central Railway of Peru, which now extends for 216 miles from the Port of Lima at Callao to Huancayo, 78 miles beyond Oroya, and in crossing the Andes reaches an altitude of 15,610ft above sea level at Ticlio (15,848ft before the Galera tunnel was bored).

The foregoing examples are isolated railway stamps in series showing other subjects as well, but they are records of railway events. Collectors will be familiar with many stamps showing locomotives, trains or other features of railway engineering which are not associated with any particular railway theme was usually chosen to represent technical progress in the countries concerned.

The first complete set of stamps commemorating a railway event came in 1908 from Ecuador, where the first railway in the country had just been completed between Guayaquil and Quito. Of the seven values in the series, the one-centavo shows a locomotive, the two, five, 10, 20 and 50 centavos are portraits, and the one-sucre is a view of Mount Chimborazo.

For the first century of railways, Britain held aloof from commemorative stamps, and although the first Wembley Exhibition stamps were produced in 1924, the Railway Centenary of 1925 went unrecorded in the stamp catalogues. The Belgian Post Office similarly passed over the centenary in 1935 of opening the railway from Brussels to Malines, which began the railway age in that country. A commemorative set was issued, however, by the Belgian National Railways for its parcels service. Ten values, from 10 cents to 90 cents, show a diesel train and the 15 values from one franc to 100 francs are of the early locomotive *Le Belge.*

From 1936, however, there was a spate of centenary issues, with pictorials ranging from early steam locomotives to the French Class 241-A, the Flying Hamburger diesel train and the latest in electric traction. In 1955, France commemorated two centenaries in a single stamp, the four-franc National Relief Fund issue recording the opening in 1843 of the lines from Paris to

Orleans and to Rousen. Its striking design sets a driver at the cab window of a modern main-line steam locomotive against a small inset of a locomotive and train of a hundred years earlier.

In North America, a 75th anniversary was commemorated in 1944 – that of the completion of the first transcontinental railway, recorded by the issue of a single three-cent stamp showing a locomotive and welcoming crowds. In Canada, the centenary of the Grand Trunk Railroad in 1951 coincided with that of the first Canadian postage stamps and the commemorative set is postal rather than railway orientated. The four-cents design shows steam- and diesel-hauled mail trains, the five-cents shows steamships, and the seven-cents stamp has a reproduction of the three-pence beaver design of the 1851 series.

South America is rich in railway commemorative

RAILWAY TRANSPORT

issues from the 1930s onwards, sometimes on lines of only local interest, although collectively such stamps do give a picture of how the railway systems in the various countries were built up. Two 1932 sets from Nicaragua commemorating the openings of the Rivas and the Leon-Sauce railways have become very rare. Each has ten values with scenes on the respective railways, representing stations and civil engineering works rather than the trains.

Egypt was the first of the countries in Africa to commemorate a railway centenary on a stamp, doing so in 1957 with a 10-milliemes design showing an early locomotive and a modern express train. South Africa followed in 1960 with a 1s 3d design showing a similar motive power contrast. Some of the newly independent countries in Africa have celebrated other railway anniversaries with special stamps, such as Ghana (60th anniversary in 1963, set of four) and Malawi (65th anniversary of railways in Basutoland, set of four, 1968). Kenya, Uganda and Tanzania issued a joint set of four stamps in 1971 to mark the fiftieth anniversary of railways in Kenya.

Among the countries of the Far East and the Pacific, Japan leads with railway anniversary commemoratives, having celebrated the 70th (1042), 75th (1947) and 100th anniversaries of its national railway system. Opening ceremonies have been recorded on stamps in that part of the world in quite recent years, including the inauguration of the JNR New Tokaido line in 1964. India, Pakistan, Australia and New Zealand have confined themselves to centenary stamps. The march of time is now bringing bicentenaries into distant view and stages on the journey have been marked with railway stamps from several countries, mainly 125th anniversaries, but Czechoslovakia in 1968 commemorated the 140th anniversary of the Ceske Budejovice-Linz railway with two stamps, one showing a horse-drawn coach on rails and the other early steam and modern electric locomotives.

In addition to commemorating national railway openings, stamps have often celebrated new links between two countries. Events of this kind have been chronicled in the stamp catalogues since 1929, when Guatemala completed its rail connection with Salvador. Sometimes both countries concerned have issued stamps, as in 1971 when Turkey and Iran celebrated the rail link between each other in this way.

About 20 railway pioneers and inventors figure on stamps of various countries. Hungary honoured both George Stephenson and its own Kalman Kando in an explorers and inventors series in 1948, which oddly enough was issued for air mails; and George turns up again in 1961 on one value of a set issued in connection with a Communication Ministers' conference. Hungary is a prolific source of stamps with railway designs. Belgium includes Walschaerts in a set put on· sale in 1955, illustrating scientists, in connection with the Cultural Fund.

Electrification schemes, new underground lines and in recent years the introduction of new locomotives have all been recorded in stamps. The last-named has been a popular theme for Russian issues, but Switzerland included the Cisalpin four-current TEE train in a publicity issue of 1962 calling attention to various Swiss events. Rail postal services also have various stages of their development represented in the stamp catalogue. The increasing number of pictorial and commemorative stamps issued all over the world is certain to give railways a better representation in their second century than they enjoyed during their first hundred years.

Building Model Railways

ABOUT SIXTY to seventy years ago, there was a mere handful of enthusiasts active in modelling the railways; now the hobby has developed to become recognised as a major pastime, although the scales commonly used in modelling have become smaller. The general interest and fascination that most men derive from the full-size railways is well known, and this usually dates back to their childhood days, which accounts for the fact that many of the model railway layouts of today are depicting the scene as it was in the days of steam, very often going back to the 1920s and sometimes beyond.

Many of the present model railway layouts have started from the toy train set laid on the floor, but they have gradually developed into a hobby that is both absorbing and comprehensive, for it embraces carpentry, metalwork, electrical wiring and miniature civil engineering, to say nothing of the artistic talents that come to the fore in the building and painting of scenery and so on. Again, the administrative talents can be used in the planning of the layout and the operation of the completed system. It is a hobby that need never be finished, for there are always further developments and improvements that could be made; possibly no other hobby can offer so much scope for individuality and ability.

As many of the model layouts developed from simple train sets, it is often the reason for a particular scale or size being chosen by the advancing modeller. Before the last war, the general scale was 7mm to 1ft, called gauge 0, but the most popular size today is 00 scale with is 4mm to 1ft, or 1/76 of full size. The 00 scale is well catered for by the proprietary and model trade and parts and accessories are fairly plentiful. Other scales are N gauge (2mm to 1ft); HO scale 3½mm to 1ft); and TT gauge (3mm to 1ft).

The newcomer to the hobby must give careful consideration to the size and scale to be used, and the actual location of the model railway layout and available space will, of course, have a bearing on the scale selected. It is preferably to have the model railway installed in a separate room, say a spare bedroom, where it can be mounted on permanent baseboards attached to the walls at a height of 3ft or so. Other situations can be a garden shed, a garage, or an attic or loft. The latter is ideal, but sufficient headroom must be available, and there is sometimes a problem in keeping it cool in the hot days of summer. In America many houses have large cellars, which again is an ideal location.

Having decided on the siting of the model railway, it is necessary to think carefully about the style of prototype to be modelled. Some people have grandiose ideas of miles of track, complicated junctions and large terminal stations that put Waterloo in the shade! Such pipe-dreams seldom come to fruition, mainly on a question of cost, the space needed, and the fact that it will take years to build before getting the fun of operating it. It is therefore far better to design a more simple layout, to get part of it working and then to develop it by stages. Early in this planning stage, one should also give thought to the particular operating company to be depicted; whether it will be one of the earlier British main-line companies, BR with its modern image, a Continental installation, a narrow-gauge line such as found in North Wales or various parts of Europe, or perhaps an industrial line. Obviously, the choice of the prototype to be followed will influence the motive power and rolling stock to be purchased or built; it can also affect the design and size of the baseboards required.

Having decided on the prototype, one has also to choose whether the layout is to be of the main-line variety, or whether it will accommodate three coaches! Each of the great variety of railway spheres of operation that can be modelled, from the largest to the smallest, can give pleasure to the operator. Many existing models of branch lines are accommodated on one or two baseboards of relatively short length and only 18in or 2ft wide; the station is generally arranged at one end with the line proceeding through a country scene to disappear into a tunnel, where it enters a fiddle-yard — often a collection of tracks mounted on a traverser which can be slid to connect any one of them with the continuous line, thus allowing a quick turn-round or substitution of stock. The fiddle-yards are usually hidden from the spectator by a tunnel or a range of hills, which will blend in with the scenery and will not spoil the illusion.

Naturally, selection of an end-to-end layout means that trains cannot be run round a continuous circle, which can also have an appeal; probably the ideal layout is a design that incorporates both conceptions. The ring layout need not be a plain circle or oval of track and it is

A scene on a gauge-0 (7mm scale) layout owned by the Gainsborough Model Railway Club. Most of the rolling stock is hand built and the emphasis is more on operation than scenery and layout. *B Monaghan*

far more interesting as a figure-of-eight rising and burrowing over and under itself. Junctions from a double-track main line can then lead to a country branch line or to terminal stations. Whatever type of layout is required, adequate planning is essential before the baseboards are constructed; the design will determine the width of the baseboards at any given position, and it is embarrassing to have them 6ft wide with only a double track and narrow scenery which needs a mere 2ft of width.

Baseboard construction is purely elementary carpentry. The top surface is best constructed with ⅜in or ½in chipboard, which is moderately rigid, comparatively inexpensive and not too heavy; further, it is easily sawn, and will take nails and screws without difficulty. It also has the advantage that it can be purchased in large sheets if necessary. The legs and supports for the baseboards should be made from 1in by 1½in hardwood, the size depending on the strength needed for the particular board, but remember that if the design necessitates bearing the weight of a human being – possibly to gain access to a window – it should be strong enough to bear such weight. The height of the baseboards must be governed by the location; in a loft they might have to be lower than normal, but wherever possible a good height is about 3ft 6in. If the layout is to be used for public exhibition, it is preferable to keep

them slightly lower so that small children can view their operation without too much difficulty. Horizontal supports for the chipboard can be strips of 1in by 1in fixed to the legs, and cross braced every 18in or so.

If the layout design has been carefully prepared, there is no need to fill in the entire area with chipboard; open-type construction can be used with advantage, with heavier chipboard laid only where the tracks are to run and the scenery built up on a lighter framework. Tracks which rise or burrow below the datum line are best constructed using the open method. There is no necessity for mitred or tongued-and-grooved joints to be made in baseboard construction; the normal butt joint, screwed and glued, is usually quite sufficient.

After completion of the baseboard, the next operation is the laying of the track-work. This is an area of many diverse thoughts which has been the subject of numerous handbooks and articles. The modern idea is to use proprietary flexible tracks, which have rails attached to plastic sleepers and can be gently bent to form the required curves. Such track can be readily purchased from most good model shops and there are several competitive makes to choose from. Trackwork points and crossings can be matched to the particular make of track, and at least some manufacturers' products are compatible with each other; but alas, that is not always the case, and enquiries should be made first.

Left: A hand-built 4mm-scale model locomotive photographed against mock wintry conditions. The model was built by Mr Lawson Little of Mansfield. *B Monaghan*

Below: A scene on the 4mm-scale model railway of Alan Bastable.

Bottom: A Tri-ang locomotive and coaches which have been modified and repainted by R Prattley of Harrogate. The scene represents part of the station on a large layout. *R Prattley*

The track is best laid on an underlay which will be a help in achieving smooth track, and also reduce the noise of the running trains. A suitable foam-rubber underlay can be purchased ready made, but it is easy to cut strips from sheets of this material about ⅛in thick such as is used for bath mats etc. Sheet cork of an equivalent thickness is also ideal. To obtain optimum realism, after the track has been laid with its underlay, it should be ballasted with fine 'granite' chippings. Simulating ballast is a perfect example of the old adage 'necessity is the mother of invention', for such items as bird seed, aquarium shingle, and even dried tea leaves have been used effectively.

There is no need to wait until all the track has been laid before operating the layout. It is better to get the main line done, with the appropriate points laid, even if the other lines are not connected — so that something can be running, even if on a temporary basis, to spur the owner to complete the remainder in easy stages. Similar remarks also apply to scenery and accessories, which can follow as time and finance allow. One of the great joys of model railways, and one of the reasons why they are seldom really complete, is that there is always something to be added or improved.

Scenery has to be made on the spot and, again, is the subject of various published writings. A popular medium is chicken wire of fine mesh, which can be stapled over wooden formers of the approximate contours required and covered with material which has been liberally soaked or painted with plaster of paris or proprietary fillers. It can then be shaped as required and, when hard, painted in the required shades. Before the paint is dry it can be spinkled with flock powders of various colours to give the effect of grass, earth etc. Cork bark can be useful for the rock faces in cuttings and other features. Trees and vegetation can be added using small twigs decorated with lichen or sponge rubber pieces stuck on and appropriately painted. All the basic materials are available from model shops and stores, and the use of such items with one's own artistic abilities can produce some very good effects.

Model buildings can be made from stiff cardboard (Bristol board), plastic sheets, then wood or sheet metal. Many models incorporate all the above materials, each used for its most appropriate purpose. A great variety of buildings in the various common modelling scales can be purchased as kits, which might need only painting; many Continental manufacturers produce injection-moulded plastics in the correct colours. The kits can be made up as prescribed, but there can be considerable pleasure from adapting parts of two or more proprietary kits to make something unique and different from the original conception. Hand-made buildings can be covered with realistic brick, tile or stone papers available from model shops for the various scales.

Apart from buildings, many lineside accessories are required, including telegraph poles, water columns, signals, buffer stops and a host of other items. They also can be purchased complete, as kits, or can be built at home. Even such items as station awnings and the fancy valancing often seen on the older type of station is available to add realism to the final structure. Miniature figures to represent railway staff and passengers in characteristic poses, are best purchased for the smaller scales, as they are too small to be adequately modelled by hand, but they make all the difference and can bring almost any desired situation to life.

As electricity is the usual form of propulsion for the smaller scales, some wiring will have to be carried out. It is now a generally accepted standard that the electric motive power supply be fed into the track at 12 volts direct current. This means that from the normal household mains a transformer and rectifier must be used, and this is generally incorporated in a controller which varies the voltage to enable the motor in the locomotive to be run at any required speed from dead slow to maximum and stopped or reversed. The modern form of transformer/controller has advanced considerably from the early days; all now incorporate metal rectifiers and many have electronic components designed to give a smooth control of output, and even to compensate for the extra power taken when a model is climbing, so that it will maintain a constant speed irrespective of gradient. Some makers incorporate switches which can be connected to different sections of the layout, so that they can be isolated or energised accordingly. Realistic running is therefore easy, and several trains on quite complex layouts can be operated simultaneously and controlled from the one unit.

With the recent advances in electric motors, particularly the permanent magnets used therein, modern motors are smaller and more powerful, and are capable of responding to every movement of the main controller. A locomotive, even in the smallest scales, can now pull a model train of 12 or 15 passenger coaches or up to 60 freight wagons if required.

The electrical side of a model railway layout can become very complicated and can incorporate many relays for semi-automatic operation, not only of the trains themselves, but also of the accessories and ancillary equipment. However, it is far better to progress slowly towards complexity, and first to get the points working by means of straightforward electrical solenoids. Point motors, and other electrical gadgets, can be purchased and many ingenious uses have been made of standard electronic gear available from radio and electrical retailers.

The choice of motive power and rolling stock is unlimited, for any prototype can be modelled and it is surprising how many plans and dimensioned drawings are available. However, some people prefer to purchase such items, devoting their abilities to other fields of railway modelling. Fortunately, due to the popularity of the hobby throughout the world, the choice is very extensive in most of the popular scales. Apart from the ready-to-run models available from the manufacturers that do service both for the toy market and the scale model enthusiast, there are several manufacturers who exist purely to make accurate scale models, often to order, and the quality of such hand-built models is reflected in the prices charged. The closer to scale and extent of incorporation of detail, the higher the cost.

The very high cost was reduced by the introduction of cast-metal kits, which have merely to be assembled and painted. White (bearing) metal is used; it is easily cast but has the disadvantage of low melting point, making the soldering of the kits a matter of difficulty to the inexperienced. Special low-melt solders and low-heat soldering irons help, but it is now more practical to use quick-setting epoxy resin adhesives, which can make a joint of great strength and be set in a matter of half an hour or less.

Many white-metal kits are available on the British market, but they have not proved so popular on the Continent; there, proprietary model locomotives with injection moulded plastics bodies incorporating all detail are more plentiful and certainly less costly than in the UK. In America there is a preponderance of good kits manufactured in the States, and imported from Japan, where the parts are cast or cut from good-quality brass or nickel-silver; a method of lost-wax casting enables the smallest detail to be incorporated in a hard durable metal.

The enthusiast who is bent on constructing his own locomotives has to work from the bare metals — a sheet of brass, nickel-silver or tinplate. The metal has to be cut to exact shapes, rolled or formed and made up to the dimensions of the boiler and other ancilliary parts. He might possibly be able to purchase suitable bogies and driving wheels, but will have to make the main frames and to fit a motor and gears. Likewise, the tender will have to be constructed from the basic materials, apart from the wheels and axles. One might be lucky and find it possible to utilise some standard parts from proprietary models or some of the castings that are available on the market, but for a model of one of the more obscure engine types, parts will have to be fabricated from scratch, perhaps even down to making patterns for castings of such parts as axleguards and so on.

What has been said about building or assembling locomotives is equally appropriate for passenger coaches and freight wagons. There is, however, one point of difference. The comparatively recent introduction of polystyrene sheet (or Plastikard, as it is known), has revolutionised the hand building of rolling stock, for it is ideal for the fabrication of coach and wagon sides, roofs and ends. Plastikard is available in sheets of varying thickness, is easily cut, drilled, sanded and filed, and can be glued using special adhesives. It takes paint well, and will not shrink, expand or warp under normal conditions. It is semi-rigid, and it is an easy matter to brace a coach side over a length of say 12in. Modern materials have made it much easier to make rolling stock nowadays than it was, say fifteen years back. As the material is light in weight it is usual to add some metal weighting in the under side, or in the body of the vehicle, although the bogie frames, if of cast metal, might give sufficient weight for stability.

Operation of a model railway, whether it is capable of utilising the services of only one operator or a team, will depend upon its design. With a large layout, it is the usual practice to install the operators in their various positions and to use correct bell code signals between them, in exactly the same way as full-size signal cabins. Timetable operation is also frequently employed and can greatly add to the enjoyment, especially if carefully planned or adapted from the working timetable of the prototype system.

Good layouts often depict a certain area and a definite period, the latter determining the style of dress of model passengers and train staff, the type of any road vehicles used in the layout and, of course, the architectural styles of the buildings and accessories. The complexity of the model railway layout can vary widely, according to the whims of the owner and builder; likewise, the emphasis can be put on any of the particular aspects — scenery, operation, or rolling stock — according to ability or fancies. Whatever is done, model railways can be an all-absorbing hobby.

Top: A station scene on the N-gauge
(2mm= 1ft) layout of the Manchester Model
Railway Society. All scenery and buildings
were hand built. *B Monaghan*

Below: Hand-built station buildings for a 4mm-
scale layout being constructed for the South
Shields Model Railway Club. The buildings
are made from wood and card, covered in stone
papers etc and painted, *B Monaghan*

Almost a Century and a half of Railway Tickets

BROADLY SPEAKING, the age of the steam railway was the age of the Edmondson card ticket. Tickets of other shapes and forms are becoming more and more common, but still to most of us a railway ticket is a piece of coloured card measuring 2¼ inches by $1\frac{3}{16}$ inches which admits us to the platform, must be safely kept throughout the journey, and is finally relinquished at the barrier at the journey's end.

The earliest railways not unnaturally looked to stage-coach practice for collecting their revenue and relied principally on waybills, which provided the guard with details of passengers entraining at each station. This was the case with the coaches operated on the Stockton & Darlington Railway in 1825-30, but as the number of passengers under the guard's care increased it became necessary to issue each passenger with a ticket showing that he had paid his fare and establishing his entitlement to travel.

Early tickets were usually in the form of slips of paper, cut from a book, on which the station clerk entered the journey details, such as time of train, fare paid and even in some cases the passenger's name. One or two companies used metal tickets, like tokens, which were collected at the destination and returned to the issuing station for re-use.

By the late 1830s the railway revolution had begun — people were travelling on a scale that could not have been conceived twenty years previously, and the laborious system of 'booking' with paper tickets was everywhere causing delays at busy stations. Worse still was its failure to provide a proper accountancy check on the station's takings.

The simple and effective answer to the problems came in 1837, the invention of a booking clerk in the North of England whose name was to become associated with railway tickets throughout the world. Thomas Edmondson was born in Lancaster in 1792 and after a somewhat chequered career as a cabinet maker entered the service of the newly opened Newcastle & Carlisle Railway as station clerk at Milton, near Carlisle, in 1836. Recognising the short-comings of the existing ticketing arrangements, Edmondson first experimented with writing out tickets on small pieces of card, a set for each station to which he had regular bookings, and with the tickets in each set progressively numbered. The next step was quantity production of the tickets on a small scale by means of a hand press, which he followed up by designing wooden racks or 'tubes' in which the tickets could be stored ready for use, and from which they could only be withdrawn one at a time and in numerical order.

Thus was laid the foundations of a system which was simple, relatively cheap and yet almost foolproof. Tickets printed by the company and issued to stations became accountable for cash, in effect on a 'sale or return' basis. To establish the day's takings the clerk had

Top: A modern BR machine-printed ticket
J E Shelbourn

Centre: BR special ticket covering period travel over a large area of Scotland during the 1970 Commonwealth Games. *J E Shelbourn*

Below: A child's first-class ticket of the Liverpool Overhead Railway around the turn of the century. *J E Shelbourn*

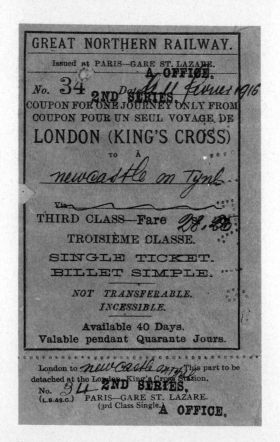

only to note the serial number of each type of ticket at the beginning and end of his shift. To the passenger the ticket became an instantly recognisable receipt, showing that he had paid his fare and franking him through his journey. The final safeguard was to ensure that it was collected from him as soon as his journey was completed, and cancelled or destroyed to prevent any possibility of re-use.

Edmondson was under no illusions as to the significance of his invention and he took out a number of patents from 1839 onwards, covering ancilliary equipment such as dating presses, ticket numbering machines and nippers. In the same year he left the Newcastle & Carlisle to join the Manchester & Leeds Railway. On that line he installed the first application of his ticket system to a complete railway, and he was appointed chief booking clerk at Manchester in time for the opening of the first section of the line in July 1839. But that was only a beginning; within about a year Edmondson set up his own ticket factory in Manchester and besides printing tickets in large quantities to order he also licensed his patents to other railway companies who wished to use the system and print their own tickets, receiving an annual royalty based on the number of miles of line operated.

By 1841 Edmondson tickets were in use on the Paris & Rouen Railway and the worldwide spread had started. Ten years later most British companies had adopted the system and railways in many other countries were producing tickets of the same familiar shape and size but in a variety of languages and typography. In a few parts of the world, especially America and the Far East, Edmondson's tickets found less general acceptance; elsewhere they have held the field for about a hundred years and it is only comparatively recently that mechanisation and automation have led to their displacement by other types of ticket on a large scale.

The earliest card tickets were characteristically simple in design and bore only the essentials — journey details, class of accommodation and a serial number. Gradually it became customary to head the ticket with the name of the issuing company. The fare paid was not generally shown until 1890, when it became a legal requirement in Britain; even then it was confined to ordinary tickets at full fare and there was no obligation to print the fare on excursion and other tickets at reduced rates.

The older paper tickets had often included a note of exhortation or warning to the passenger — *Please to hold this Ticket till called for* (Stockton & Darlington Railway); *Provided there be room in the Carriages on arrival* (Grand Junction Railway) or the reminder that *No fees or gratuities are allowed to be taken by the Company's servants*. At first there was no room for such legends on the rather crudely printed Edmondson tickets, but by the 1860s there was frequently a brief reference to the Company's bye-laws and conditions upon which tickets

Top: A modern BR card season ticket valid for travel over a complete zone. *J E Shelbourn*

Centre: An 1883 hand-written half-fare ticket of the American Richmond & Danville Railroad. *J E Shelbourn*

Below: Ticket issued at Paris Gare St Lazare station for a journey in Britain from London to Newcastle in 1916. *J E Shelbourn*

were issued. This became standard practice and indeed tickets for through bookings over 'foreign' lines carried a lengthy statement as to the liability or otherwise of the companies concerned for 'loss, damage or delay however caused'. This, like the conditions and validity of modern British tickets, was printed on the back of the ticket.

Return tickets were originally very similar to singles, with the words 'and back' added to the journey details, but for through bookings over the lines of two companies it was necessary for the second company to retain some evidence of the journey made, in order to claim the appropriate portion of the fare. This led to the well-known two-coupon type of return ticket in which one half is given up at the end of the outward journey, the other half being retained for the return journey. This type of return was for many years almost universal in Britain, but railways in other parts of the world often favoured the single-coupon 'and back' type.

Colour has always been an important feature in the design of tickets. From the earliest days it has been used to denote the class of accommodation paid for — an obvious aid to ticket inspection — and most British railways settled down to a convention whereby ordinary first-class tickets were white, second-class pink or blue and third-class buff or green. But there were exceptions which gave a kaleidoscopic effect in pre-grouping days — Great Northern third-class tickets were blue for instance, while those of the London & South Western were pink. Excursion tickets were often multi-coloured, or printed with one, two or three red stripes to denote the class. For a time the Great Eastern Railway coloured tickets according to the direction of travel, an ingenious method of assisting the ticket collector on busy suburban lines. Thus all third-class passengers arriving by, say, a down train at Ilford would be expected to hold green tickets, and anyone proffering a buff ticket (the up-direction colour) would be immediately suspect. Nowadays BR tickets are uniformly white for first class and green for second class, an unfortunate clash with practice on the European mainland where by international agreement green denotes first class and second-class tickets are brown.

On most railway systems children under a specified age (usually 12 or 14) are conveyed at half fare, which necessitates special ticketing arrangements. For bookings where there is a steady demand, separate stocks of tickets are held, with the world 'child' either overprinted or incorporated in the text. In other cases full-fare tickets are used and cut in half for issue to children, which simplifies accountancy but means that the essential details on the ticket must be repeated so that they appear on each half when the ticket is bisected. Another method, formerly used in this country and still common elsewhere, involves cutting off a small identifiable portion of the ticket. The ticket thus mutilated is readily recognised as a child issue, and the severed portion is returned to the audit office in lieu of cash to account for the other half of the normal fare.

A large proportion of passenger journeys are made at reduced fares and this gives rise to an enormous variety of tickets. Cheap fares are basically of two kinds. First there are those generally available to all travellers, but subject to restricted validity, usually of date or time. Into this category fall most excursion, cheap day, weekend etc tickets, typical examples being the modern off-peak tickets, and excursion tickets for particular occasions or events which might be available only on specified train services.

The second type of cheap ticket consists of those issued to particular categories of passenger. Commonest among them are privilege tickets (for railwaymen and their families), workmen's tickets (originally for bona fide workmen, but later generally available as early morning returns) and tickets for members of the armed forces and mercantile marine on leave. In France there are reduced rates for *mutiles de guerre* (war wounded). But this by no means exhausts the possibilities; there have been specially printed tickets for anglers, drovers, members of theatrical companies, shipwrecked mariners and many others.

All the tickets so far mentioned are for passenger travel by train, but railways issue a variety of tickets for ancilliary services and other purposes. Through bookings are available by rail and ship, rail and bus, or even by all three on the same ticket. Familiar examples of non-travel tickets are platform tickets, car parking tickets (for station car parks) and supplementary tickets for accommodation in Pullmans, sleepers and observation cars. Less well known perhaps are tickets for *One load of Native Produce, accompanying passenger* (East African Railways) or *Conveyance of one Motor Car through the Severn Tunnel* (Great Western Railway). On the Highland Railway, and its successors down to quite recent times, there were passenger tickets available by goods train — at first-class fare! There are also many railway-issued tickets for ferries, toll bridges, pier dues and the like.

Almost all of the many varied requirements have been met by the ubiquitous Edmondson card, but there have always been certain facilities for which other forms of ticket were more suitable. Non-Edmondson tickets in what might be termed the classical period (before the machine era) were generally of three kinds:

(a) Most railways used large paper tickets, with some details filled in by hand, for unusual bookings, special parties and other purposes for which printed stock was not justified. Paper tickets are also common on American railroads.

(b) Season tickets, contracts and passes have existed from the earliest days, generally in the form of cards considerably larger than Edmondson size, sometimes folded and covered in cloth or even leather bound.

(c) When steam railmotor services were introduced early in this century, conductors on the trains issued bell-punch tickets very similar to those used on the buses and trams with which the railmotors were intended to compete. Punch-type tickets were largely a British institution — elsewhere pads of paper tickets served the same purpose.

The first large-scale application of mechanisation to ticket issue was on urban systems where an intensive demand for tickets was associated with cramped conditions in booking offices, often situated underground. The Paris Metropolitain, with a flat fare and relatively few different tickets required at each station, installed ticket-issuing machines from the opening of its first line in 1900. The London Underground lines, which had previously used conventional Edmondson cards, followed suit soon afterwards, at first with pull-bar

Facing page: A selection of tickets of various types from several countries. J E Shelbourn Collection

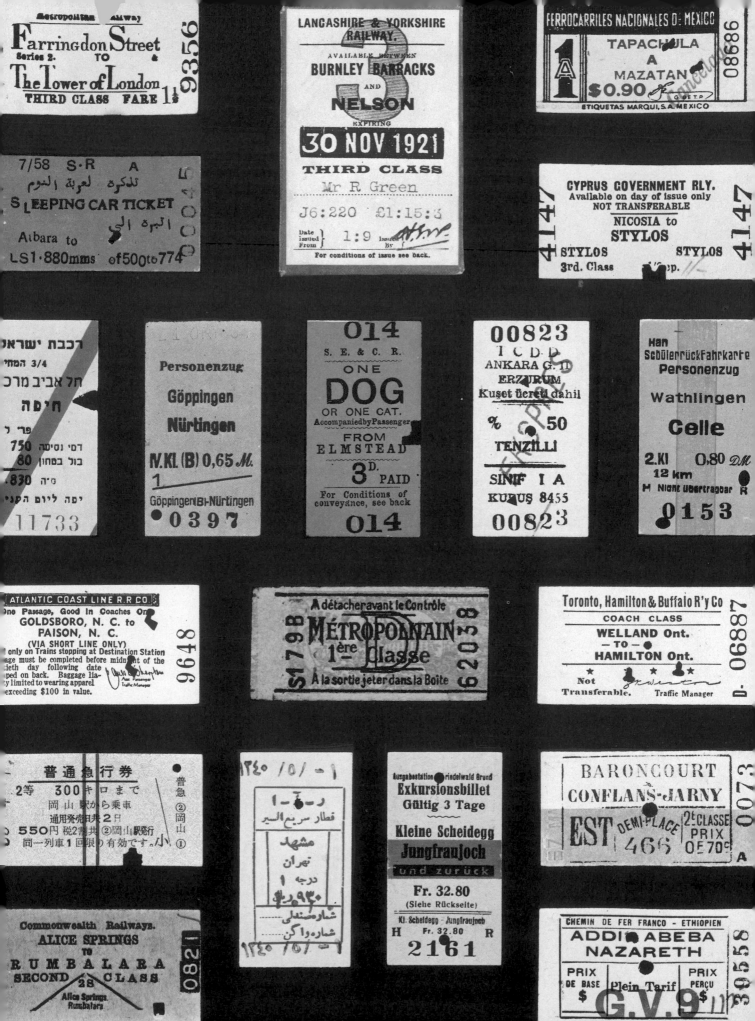

machines stocked with pre-printed tickets, later with machines which actually printed tickets at the moment of issue like those in Paris.

The use of point-of-sale ticket-printing machines was a great step forward, at once doing away with expensive stocks of printed tickets and at the same time providing a running cash total for all tickets issued. A German machine suitable for large stations on main-line railways, capable of printing a wide range of tickets by simple selection from plates stored in the machine, was tried on the Prussian State Railways in 1907. It was subsequently developed and became widely used on the Continent, and was the forerunner of British Railways multiprinter and flexiprinter machines now installed at a number of principal stations. These machines print tickets on Edmondson-size cards, the colour being selected according to the type of ticket required.

Machines of the 'rapidprinter' type, well known on London Transport, produce tickets on card thinner and somewhat longer than Edmondson's, the ticket being cut off from a roll of card after printing. Each machine of this type prints one type of ticket only; automatic (coin-operated) machines consist of a single unit, but in booking offices a number of units are mounted side by side. For on-train issues, portable machines printing paper tickets are coming into common use, and here again the railways have adopted a variety of machines already used by bus operators, as well as others specifically designed for railway use.

Yet another principle has added to the bewildering variety of tickets in recent years. In some respects it is a compromise, in that pre-printed tickets are retained but they require validation in a cash register type of machine when issued. The system adopted by Southern Region of British Rail uses specially designed Edmondson cards for the purpose. More striking are the Hugin tickets now in use at some British Railways stations; they are large cards printed in red or black with a space for machine validation at one end. The machine provides a magnetic tape for audit and statistical analysis.

The latest stage in automation of fare collection is the automatic inspection of tickets. Entry or exit barriers able to 'read' magnetically coded tickets first appeared in 1964 on the Long Island Railroad in the USA, and at one or two London Transport stations. Shortly afterwards two stations on the Paris Metro were similarly equipped, and electronic tickets are now in use on the Milan Underground. The coding is done at the time of issue and is embodied in a brown oxide coating or strip on the back of the ticket. Problems remain to be solved and so far the new systems operate alongside conventional ticketing arrangements. But the day might not be far off when we shall see a completely closed system in which electronic tickets are issued, inspected and finally collected without the need for any staff at all.

Top: Krauss-built 1882 0-6-0T locomotive for Hungary, on outside exhibition in Budapest. *D Williamson*

Centre: Dubs-built (British) 1891 0-4-0T crane for Argentina on show at Buenos Aires Retiro station. *C & D Gannon*

Bottom: White Mountain Central Railroad Heisler 1926 double 0-4-0 on exhibition at Clarke's Trading Post in the US. *D T Rowe*

Facing page: LMS 4-6-2 No 6201 'Princess Elizabeth' in steam (on loan for an open-day) at the Birmingham Railway Museum at Tyseley. *J Adams*

Railway Museums

CIVILISED MAN has long been accustomed to collect around him artefacts illustrating various aspects of his history for the purpose of edifying his children. The invention of the railway — and in particular the steam locomotive — was such an epoch-making event it was inevitable that, sooner or later, collections of railway relics would be established. Indeed it is surprising that they were not established sooner. In the early years of railways, half-hearted attempts were made by designers to preserve significant items, for example the famous *North Star* of the Great Western, but many were ruthlessly scrapped by their successors. It was not until the end of the nineteenth century that a few far-sighted men started on a small scale to organise national collections of railwayana, and serious widespread preservation had to wait until after the second world war, when it was almost too late.

The first attempt to form a real national collection of transport relics was undertaken in Austria in 1870. In that year Baron Von Büschmann, a senior railway officer in the Ministry of Transport, produced a directive requiring — not merely requesting — all railways in the country to forward to him any items likely to be of historical importance. The edict applied to both state and private railways and the result was a collection that grew so quickly it was impossible to display it all. Nevertheless a considerable display was opened to the public in 1918 and ever since then Austria has been among the foremost countries in preserving and displaying railway relics. The present collection at the impressive Technisches Museum at Schönbrunn near Vienna, is representative of all main types and periods of railway material and there is much more in store that cannot be displayed because of lack of room.

Austria in some respects also set the pattern for museum development elsewhere; a number of countries incorporated a 'railway section' in their national museums of science and industry. Germany with the Deutsches Museum at Munich, England with the Science Museum in London, and Italy with the National Museum of Science and Technology in Milan, all provided some space for notable equipment and achievements in the railway field. Inevitably, however, only a few exhibits could be thus housed and most European countries at any rate have also developed more specialised collections of their own. Hungary, as might be expected from her association with Austria, was one of the first in 1896 but Norway (1896), Finland (1898) and Germany (1899) followed in quick succession and other countries were not far behind.

The first world war naturally upset many plans but during the 1920s and '30s numerous collections developed. Some, like the English York Railway Museum and the Saxon State Railways Museum at Dresden, were regional or even devoted to single railway companies. Others, like the German Verkehrsmuseum at Nuremburg were national collections borne upwards on a surge of pride in national achievements. Serious museum development was, oddly enough, confined at that time almost entirely to the European sub-continent and many museums showed a lack of balance in their exhibits. There was a tendency to show, in full size, only very early items, and examples of the latest and best

trains. Formative years, from the 1880s up to about 1914, were often illustrated merely by models.

What changed all this was the very considerable rise in amateur interest which occurred shortly after the second world war. Perhaps it was a return to nostalgia, perhaps a realisation that so much had been destroyed; certainly railways suddenly came under pressure to preserve a representative cross-section of their existing equipment and interesting items of earlier date were ferreted out from all sorts of hiding places.

Decaying coach bodies serving as hutments in goods yards and elsewhere were recognised as illustrating important steps in rolling-stock development; wheezing locomotives casually sold out of service to industrial firms suddenly assumed a new importance. Countries such as Switzerland and Britain, which had never had truly national railway collections, were prodded into some sort of action. Even the SNCF in France, which up to then had not appeared history-conscious, started storing away interesting locomotives and stock and then blossomed out with an 'historic train' drawn by no less a machine than its very historic Crampton.

The result in Europe has been the establishment and development in almost every country of a national collection, though often major items are not on display. To earmark equipment for preservation is comparatively easy since all that is forfeited is its scrap value. The main problem is the provision of sufficient funds to restore, house and maintain the relics, and in that respect official help and guidance is often lacking or even negatively applied. As in Great Britain, the major nationalised railways are charged with operating as commercial enterprises, and they often grudge the money for what to them is a loss-making activity. In consequence, while there is a considerable amateur interest in most European countries at any rate, the ways in which the interest is interpreted vary widely.

Britain is an excellent example of the dilemma. British Railways went so far as to appoint a Curator of historic relics and, in concert with other bodies, to establish a national transport collection at Clapham in London – supplementing that at York. Amateur bodies got together to form an advisory panel, a representative collection of items being held back from scrapping on their recommendations, while other amateur bodies actually purchased and restored equipment. As a result there is in Britain a probably unrivalled selection of historic full-size items representing all companies and all stages of development.

At the same time there is no national co-ordinating policy. The national collection itself, partly on display but with a great proportion in store, has become a political pawn. Some people argue as a matter of doctrine that such collections should be moved away from the capital to enlighten the regions. Others, while doubtful of this theory, are unwilling to pay the considerable price of rehousing the full collection on a central site and making proper provision for archives. As a result the potentially superb collection is likely to be split up into small packets. Already some items are on loan to private museums as the only way of preventing them deteriorating further, and the practice is likely to increase.

Britain is by no means alone in this dilemma; in the pioneer country, Austria, for example, many large items are rusting away for want of funds to restore and house

them. Yet most European countries are actively encouraging their national museums, and perhaps the most hopeful are those where redundant railway facilities have been taken over to provide a basis. One of the main problems for the more well-established collections has always been the difficulty of expanding their buildings, which are usually built in monumental style and in restricted grounds. A railway depot or station on the other hand usually has a considerable acreage attached and available for future expansion, while the ambience is naturally, considerably more authentic.

A disused railway location can, of course have its attendant disadvantages, as has the Dutch museum established in the old Maliebaan station in Utrecht. The big buildings allow ample space for small exhibits and an overall roof shelters most of the preserved locomotives, but much stock has to stand in the open goods yard. Consequently maintenance costs are greatly increased. Perhaps the Swedish idea, where an old double-round-house at Gavle has been taken over, is better. There each major item can have its own 'stall: while the turntables and rail connections allow individual items to be pulled out easily if required for special duties or photography.

The most recent national museum, that of France, is adopting the same policy and basing itself on the old depot of Mulhouse Nord. Those charged with its establishment have introduced an additional pleasant idea; the SNCF has always encouraged healthy competi-

Above: The King's day saloon of the 1903 train built by the LNWR for long Royal journeys; this coach is also preserved at Clapham. *C & W Meadway*

tiveness among its staff and selected depots have been given the privilege of restoring individual items of equipment. The results are superb, depot vying with depot to turn out locomotives in immaculate condition.

As an alternative, there is much to be said for the Norwegian idea of laying out its exhibits in a park, with a full-size section of line complete with representative buildings and lineside fittings. There the more delicate items of locomotives and stock can be kept under cover in properly heated premises but can be moved outside on special occasions. As an added attraction a narrow-gauge line is laid out within the grounds as an operating museum, but again the cost is high.

The cost to the corporate or national exchequer of restoring and housing items of equipment has often meant that many more historical relics are retained, or earmarked, for preservation than can conveniently be dealt with. Hence most national 'collections' include large items that are simply stored in derelict railway sheds, slowly deteriorating. In England especially, but also in other countries to a lesser extent, two partial solutions have been found — and found rather grudgingly, considering the alternatives. Most commonly, individual items have been offered on permanent loan to provincial or municipal museums trying to build up a transport section; thus Midland Railway engines were allocated to Leicester Museum, while Swindon set up a small but genuine Great Western Museum to honour the railway that gave the town birth. By this means the restoration and maintenance of precious relics is assured,

Left and above: Details of Queen Victoria's coach of 1869, preserved in the Museum of British Transport, Clapham. *J Benton-Harris*

but they are not usually grouped with others in a representative collection.

The same criticism of isolation applies to the second solution, whereby relics — locomotives and rolling stock in particular — are loaned to existing enthusiast organisations to build up collections they already have.

The most important thing in farming out worthy items to fostering organisations is to ensure that the relics are secured for a reasonably long period and not allowed to deteriorate further, as has been known to happen. In Britain some measure of co-ordination has been achieved by the independent Transport Trust, which allocates offered items to suitable homes (for example, the Bressingham Museum) and keeps a watchful eye on them. Abroad the position varies widely. In Belgium for instance all secondary railway material is held in trust by an amateur society, L'Association pour la Musee du Tramway (AMUTRA), but is first restored with the aid of public funds and housed in a former tram depot; such a museum is in effect a national collection. In France on the other hand, preservation of relics from the former vast spread of secondary railways is entirely in the hands of enthusiast bodies and lack of funds for transporting and housing exhibits has meant the scrapping or deterioration of various valuable items. The problem remains that unless some public provision is made, amateur funds are never sufficient to acquire and restore the relics available at any one time.

At their best, the enthusiast group-run museums can be very valuable to historians particularly those that have been initiated by enthusiasts to cover specialised aspects of rail transport. An excellent example is the Narrow-Gauge museum at Towyn in Wales, which has its own board of trustees and has set out successfully to provide a wide and representative range of exhibits dealing with the British narrow gauge and in particular those lines associated with the Welsh slate industry. Unfortunately many so-called enthusiast-run museums are the work of either individuals or small groups, well-intentioned but with few resources; they frequently end up as decaying collections of motley items — a small

locomotive or two, a few sad signals, some lineside relics which might even be scrapped when their owners die or lose interest.

It is often difficult in any case to decide when an amateur effort actually becomes a museum. Although outside the scope of this article, it could be claimed that most of the preserved railways and steam depots are working museums. Certainly in many cases great care is taken to restore locomotives and stock to their original state and in some instances a small museum is attached as an extra attraction. The French 60cm-gauge line at Pithiviers, for example, actually calls itself a musee vivante (living museum) and is slowly building up a collection of general secondary railway interest. Places as far apart as Steamtown in the United States of America and the Steam Locomotive Trust at Tyseley in England are really 'period settings' in which to display restored locomotives.

Indeed, if display of restored historical items is the main criterion for a museum, one further aspect of museums must be noted. This is the increasing tendency, particularly abroad, to restore redundant locomotives and vehicles and scatter them around the countryside on plinths as decoration — a process usually known by the more sardonic enthusiasts as 'stuffing'. While a single item might not make a museum, several presumably do; the American mid-west is littered with clumps of relics from dead-and-gone Colorado narrow-gauge lines, each little dusty group acting both as a tourist attraction and as a local reminder of past glories. In the same way, in Austria for instance, a small collection of vehicles from the former narrow-gauge Salzkammergutlokalbahn adorns the forecourt of a local inn and is kept in fair condition, while odd locomotives from the national museum collection have been set up in various places as outdoor exhibits.

Lastly there are the private collections such as the Tram-Museum in Holland, set up by private collectors but accessible to the public at selected times. They run the same dangers as the more rickety enthusiast-run ventures, in that the collected items are at risk if their owner dies or loses interest.

Left: A Dean goods
No 2516 and 'City of
Truro' No 3717 at the GWR
Museum, Swindon
R C Nash

Below: A 1941 Alco
4-8-8-4 of Union Pacific
at Steamtown in the
United States. *D T Rowe*

Left: Union Pacific
Northern-class 4-8-4, a
6,600hp diesel and the
preserved Rogers 4-4-0
No 119 at Ogden for the
UP Centennial in 1969.
Union Pacific Railroad

Above: Talyllyn
Railways 0-4-0
lòcomotive 'Dolgoch'
built in 1895. *John Adams*

Left: Fairbourne Railway's
'Sian'. *P B Whitehouse*

TRAINS AND RAILWAYS FOR PLEASURE

Great Little Trains of Wales

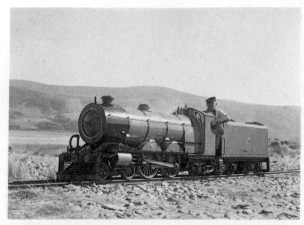

Fairbourne Railways 15in-gauge locomotive 'Count Louis'. *John Adams*

Festiniog Railway's double Fairlie locomotives 'Merddyn Emrys' at Dduallt and 'Earl of Merioneth' at Portmadoc Welshpool & Llanfair Railway's 0-6-0T No 1 'The Earl' leading No 2 'The Countess'. *C M Whitehouse*

Some Standard Gauge Tourist Railways

Severn Valley Railway

Above: Stanier Black Five Preservation Society's No 45110 on the SVR at Bridgnorth. *J Hunt*

Below: LMS Ivatt 2-6-0 No 46443 (Crewe 1950) leaving Hampton Loade in August 1971. *A G Bending*

The
Bluebell
Line

Representative of a class of 70-odd Adams 4-4-2T
engines on the London & South Western Railway
from 1882, No 488 had various owners and numbers
until it was bought after withdrawal by BR (No 30583)
in 1961 by the Bluebell Line, where it now works in
LSWR 1918 livery. *M Pope*

THE DART VALLEY · RAILWAY ·

DART VALLEY

Ex-BR 0-6-0 PT No 1638 at Buckfastleigh
C J Gammell

The Keighley & Worth Valley Light Railway

Above left: Stanier LMS Class 5 4-6-0 No 5025 at Oakworth in September 1970. *R Lush*

Above right: Gresley GNR 0-6-2T, later LNER Class N2 No 4744, shunting at Haworth yard in March 1970. *R Lush*

Below: One of the KWVR's WD 0-6-0ST engines No 63, leaving Mytholmes tunnel in April 1970. *R Lush*

Big Engines in Preservation

Flying Scotsman Preserved: Running with her double tender, the famous engine takes an enthusiasts special up Holloway Bank just outside King's Cross London. *B A Reeves*

WR No 7029 'Clun Castle' at York in August 1967.
R Bastin

Preserved LMS Jubilee-class 4-6-0 No 5596 'Bahamas' at Leeds in March 1968. *R Bastin*

Preserved Great Western Railway
4-6-0 King class locomotive No 6000
'King George V' of 1927, in steam on
BR in 1971 hauling preserved Pullman
stock. KGV is on loan to the Bulmer
cider company at Hereford by Swindon
Corporation, into whose charge it was
passed for preservation after
withdrawal from BR service in 1962.
V C K Allen

Miniature Passenger Railways

SINCE THE END of regular steam working on British Railways standard-gauge lines, the only places in Britain where steam locomotives can still be seen in action are on the various preserved lines or, in much smaller scale, the passenger-carrying miniature railways at seaside resorts, stately homes, parks and other amusement centres. Miniature railways are in a class of their own for, generally speaking, they are working models on a much smaller scale of full-size locomotives. Everything on the locomotive is a small-scale reproduction of the same item on the full-size engine, but allowance has to be made for the fact that coal, fire, water and steam cannot be reduced in scale, and certain parts, particularly those carrying steam under pressure, must be almost as strong on the model as in full size and therefore perhaps larger in size than the scale of the model demands.

Therein perhaps lies the main difference between a model locomotive and a miniature locomotive. Broadly speaking, the difference is one of terminology: *miniature* locomotives are normally used on passenger-carrying lines, but *models* are the small reproductions found on the average indoor model railway. Where detail components are added merely for show and not for working, they can be finely made, but the same item of equipment on a working miniature locomotive, perhaps carrying steam at a pressure of 10lb per sq in or more, clearly not only has to be strong enough to stand the use

Above: Typical of the small-gauge passenger carrying miniature railways is the mixed-gauge line in Blenheim Park, Woodstock, with a 5in gauge LMS class 5 4-6-0 in action. *R C H Nash*

Centre: One of the famous Bassett-Lowke Little Giant type 4-4-2 15in-gauge locomotives built for seaside lines from the turn of the century until the First World War. This was the one at Southport. A few of these engines survive today.

Below: Intermediate in size and probably the most popular commercial gauge today is 10¼ in, such as this line at Hastings. *G M Kichenside*

Right: A 15in-gauge 4-4-2, one of a pair built by Hunt of Oldbury, for the mile-long Sutton Coldfield Railway and seen here on trial on the Romney, Hythe & Dymchurch line in 1959. *George Barlow*

for which it was designed but also to withstand the wear and tear of commercial life if it is in everyday use.

There is also a difference between miniature and narrow-gauge railways; miniature railways are usually operated with locomotives whose general design and appearance is based on that of full-size main-line locomotives, and are simply replicas, a quarter or an eighth or whatever scale reduction is used, depending on gauge, of the size of the original locomotive. Narrow-gauge locomotives on the other hand are full-size locomotives, but run on tracks narrower than the standard gauge and are thus narrower and not so tall as. their standard-gauge relations. Generally the term 'miniature railway' embraces track gauges between 7¼in and 20in, anything larger coming within the realm of narrow gauge.

At the smaller end of the scale, there are passenger-carrying gauges smaller than 7¼in, for example, 2½, 3¾in and 5in gauges, but they are not normally used for commercial operation and are the favoured sizes of model engineering societies and clubs. Because of the smallness of the gauge, the tracks are

him to have his feet inside the tender or the locomotive, and his feet rest on a crossbar outside the tender. Models for 7¼in gauge are normally built to a scale of 1½in to 1ft and are thus one eighth full size. The next size up, although it is not a very popular gauge today, is 9½in, for which the models are built to 2in to 1ft scale and are thus one-sixth full size. Although this size was popular in the early years of the present century, in recent years it has been overtaken by the next larger size, 10¼in gauge which uses a scale of 2¼in to 1ft. Indeed, 10¼in gauge is undoubtedly the most popular size for commercial railways at seaside resorts, parks and other amusement centres since it will permit coaches wide enough to carry two children or an adult and child side by side, but the running expenses are very much less than with larger gauges.

Although there are few 12in-gauge miniature railways today the next most popular size is, or used to be, 15in gauge using 3in to 1ft for the scale of the locomotives. At one time, this was the most popular passenger-carrying size for pleasure railways and a considerable number of 15in gauge lines were built at the turn of the

usually raised about 2ft or so above the ground, and passengers sit astride specially designed coaches with footrests suspended from the coach below track level. By its very construction, this sort of track cannot have points in the normal sense of the term and can only have large movable sections of line to switch locomotives from one track to another. Consequently the very narrow-gauge type of railway can only be simple in form and does not really come within the normally accepted term of a commercial miniature railway.

The smallest practicable size for carrying passengers on lines at ground level is 7¼in gauge, where the passengers can sit in the coaches rather than astride them, although the latter type may occasionally be seen on this gauge. The driver normally sits on the tender of the locomotive but the cab is not usually big enough for

century; most lines of this size in existence today are survivals from that period, at least so far as seaside resort or park lines are concerned. Unfortunately, rapidly rising running and maintenance costs today are fast making lines of this size uneconomic as commercial propositions and many have closed down in recent years. However, 15in gauge is large enough to have completely enclosed coaches and since some of the more powerful locomotives can haul trainloads of a hundred or so passengers at speed of up to 20mph or more, this size of line can also be used as a means of commercial transport; two lines, the 14-mile-long Romney, Hythe & Dymchurch Railway in Kent and the 7-mile Ravenglass & Eskdale Railway in Cumberland are probably the most famous railways using 15in gauge in the world.

The Ravenglass & Eskdale Railway has a long history

but, then so have miniature railways in general. The first miniatures are as old as railways themselves, for in the pioneering days of the Stephenson-type railway in the 1820s and 30s, some engineers built models to try out new ideas before embarking on full-size locomotives, while others, having built successful steam locomotives, used demonstration models to assist sales. While many were static models, some of them worked and a few have survived to the present time in private collections and museums.

The true history of the miniature railway really starts from the 1870s. It was at that time that an amateur engineer with a love of railways, Arthur Heywood, started experiments to find out what would be the smallest practicable size of railway for transport on private estates, and even possibly for the army, as an alternative to the horse. It must be remembered that at that time, although full-size railways had become the established means of transport from one town to another, the horse was still supreme for transport of both passengers and goods for local journeys where there were no railways. It is true that standard- and narrow-gauge mineral tramways and wagonways had been used from the start of the industrial revolution for the movement of stone, coal and other minerals from working faces to rivers, ports and, in later years, railway depots, but the horse and cart was still the main form of transport away from industrial centres.

It might have been possible, for example, to use a narrow-gauge or miniature railway for the transport of crops to the nearest main railway station, or for the delivery of coal and other essentials for the running of an estate from the nearest local station. Arthur Heywood found that the smallest usable size of miniature railway suitable for the transport of goods and passengers was one with a gauge of 15 inches. He built a 15in-gauge line in the grounds of Duffield Bank, near Derby, in the 1870s, and it provided a severe test for the locomotives for it included a gradient of 1 in 10 and curves as sharp as 25ft radius. By the 1890s, Heywood's line not only had open passenger coaches but included a dining car and a sleeping car, both highly amusing luxuries for a line no more than a mile or so in length Nevertheless, it was a useful pioneering exercise to show just what could be accomplished on the 15in gauge.

In 1895, following a visit by representatives of the Duke of Westminster who owned an estate at Eaton Hall, near Chester, Arthur Heywood was asked to build a three-mile line to link the estate with the nearby GWR Balderton station. On neither the Duffield Bank nor Eaton Hall railways was there any attempt to have scale-model motive power, and the locomotives were largely four- or six-coupled tank locomotives similar in style to industrial types.

Miniature railways were by that time becoming popular overseas and in America, the firm of Cagney Brothers produced locomotive for use on amusement park lines in America and in other parts of the world. They were largely of 15in gauge but some were as small as $12\frac{5}{8}$in gauge and others as large as 22in gauge. The Cagney locomotives were ruggedly built and although based on an American prototype 4-4-0 were only loosely scale models, as they were intended for use rather than exhibition. As a result some of the engines, now more than 70 years old, are still in existence. Another notable British 15 gauge miniature railway of the period, and one on which an imported Cagney locomotive operated,

124

Top and below: The most popular gauge for private miniature railways is 7¼in and the smallest practicable size for ground-level lines. An LMS Royal Scot locomotive, built to 1/8th scale, operates on the Great Cockrow Railway near Chertsey, a line which is noted for its signalling system. *G M Kichenside*

was the Blakesley Hall Railway near Towcester, which linked the private estate to the nearby Blakesley station on the Stratford-on-Avon & Midland Junction Railway.

It was at that time, too, that the name of Bassett-Lowke became part of the British miniature railway scene. W. J. Bassett-Lowke whose famous firm was already turning out model locomotives for indoor and garden use in the small scales, far superior to the crude toys which had passed for model locomotives until the 1890s, turned his attention to the larger gauges and formed the firm of Miniature Railways Ltd in conjunction with Henry Greenly, an engineer well versed in model and miniature locomotive engineering practice. The new firm was established not only to build miniature locomotives but also to install complete railways and when finished to operate them in conjunction with the owners of the sites on a concession basis. Like Heywood before them, Bassett-Lowke and Greenly felt that 15in gauge offered all-round advantages for commercial railways and built several lines of that size between 1900 and the 1914-18 war. A basically standard locomotive was produced, using the 4-4-2 (Atlantic) wheel arrangement, of freelance design but providing a type with good steaming capacity, power, and usable weight, yet having a short coupled wheel base allowing the negotiation of relatively sharp curves. This engine, known as *Little Giant,* formed the basis for a number of other locomotives which although generally similar, varied in detail. While most of the locomotives are no longer in existence, some have survived and are now more than 60 years old.

Centre: One of the American Cagney 4-4-0 15in-gauge locomotives built in large numbers in America for amusement park lines; this one ran on the Blakesley Hall railway near Towcester, in England. *Ian Allan Library*

Bottom right: One of the Ian Allan Miniature Railway Supplies Ltd 10¼in-gauge diesels of the Meteor class used at a number of seaside resorts today. This one is at Bognor Regis.

Miniature Railways Ltd built a number of 15in-gauge lines at seaside resorts round the country and at exhibition sites. Even then, in the years just before the first world war, it was becoming apparent that the 15in gauge was rather an expensive luxury for short-distance seaside and amusement park pleasure lines. In 1911 Miniature Railways Ltd was wound up and although a new company — Narrow Gauge Railways Ltd — was formed by Bassett-Lowke for marketing 15in-gauge equipment, it concentrated on producing equipment for longer-distance lines and no longer operated lines itself. One of the lines in which Narrow Gauge Railways was interested was the Ravenglass & Eskdale in Cumberland, originally built in 1875 with a gauge of 3ft to carry minerals from Boot to the port of Ravenglass on the coast. By the outbreak of war in 1914 the line had become derelict and Narrow Gauge Railways sought to explore the possibility of converting it to 15in gauge as a recreational line for passengers and the small amount of potential freight that still existed. Another line taken over by Narrow Gauge Railways Ltd during the first world war was the Fairbourne Railway, which had started life as a 2ft-gauge industrial concern carrying building materials for housing development at Fairbourne. The gauge was narrowed to 15in and it, too, became a pleasure line, although much shorter than the Ravenglass & Eskdale.

During the middle 1920s, Narrow Gauge Railways Ltd changed hands; Bassett-Lowke no longer had any connection with the building or operation of complete railways although his firm still supplied miniature railway locomotives, but no longer in 15in gauge. Henry Greenly, on the other hand, was kept busy on miniature railway design for he became Engineer of what was undoubtedly the most ambitious 15in-gauge railway ever built — the Romney, Hythe & Dymchurch Railway on the south coast of Kent. It was opened in 1927 between Hythe and New Romney and was later extended southwards to Dungeness Point, giving a total route length of 14 miles. Although a track gauge of 15in was adopted, the locomotives were built to a scale of 4in to 1ft, that is one-third full size, instead of the quarter full size normally used for this gauge. This means that the locomotives have a slightly narrow-gauge appearance, for the boilers and footplating overhang the wheels more than on an exact scale model. The Romney engines are massive machines weighing about 8 tons apiece; five of them are based on Gresley's LNER Class A1 Pacific design of 1922, the *Flying Scotsman* type. Of the remaining four locomotives, two are 4-8-2s, the only locomotives of this wheel arrangement to run in normal commercial passenger service on any gauge in Great Britain, and two are Pacific locomotives based on Canadian types.

The Romney, Hythe & Dymchurch Railway was distinguished by being built and operated under a Light Railway Order issued by the Ministry of Transport, an official procedure normally not necessary with railways so small, but required in this instance since it was to be a public railway. Indeed, the RHDR rightly claims the title of the smallest public railway in the world. All three of these 15in gauge railways — the Fairbourne, the Ravenglass & Eskdale, and the Romney, Hythe & Dymchurch — survive today, although with changing fortunes in the intervening years; both the latter might have disappeared before now had it not been for the help of preservation societies and railway enthusiasts

Above: Undoubtedly the most famous 15in-gauge railway 'the smallest public railway in the world' is the Romney, Hythe & Dymchurch Railway in Kent. One of the lines 4-6-2s, No 1, stands waiting to leave Hythe with a train for Dungeness in summer 1971. *G R Hounsell*

Right: R & E 0-8-2 'River Irt' heading a train for Dalegarth out of Eskdale Green. *J A Ingram*

who have taken over the operation of the two lines as part of the general railway preservation movement of branch and narrow-gauge lines in the 1960s and 70s.

During the last 40 years numerous 10¼in and 7¼in-gauge lines have been built at seaside resorts, public parks and on private estates, and for exhibition purposes. The 1924/5 Wembley Exhibition included a 9½in-gauge miniature railway which was powered by a scale replica of a Great Northern Atlantic. This engine had the distinction of hauling King George V and Queen Mary when they visited the exhibition; the engine itself survives today, rebuilt to the 10¼in gauge at Bressingham Hall, near Diss, in Norfolk. Bressingham has become a home for retired steam and houses an interesting collection of railways and miniature railways. Part of its attraction is a short length of standard-gauge line on which full-size locomotives can be run and several miniature and narrow-gauge lines.

Although the days of the privately owned estate railway, probably financed by a wealthy railway enthusiast owner, are virtually over, several stately homes have continued or installed new miniature railways as part of the general amenities to attract visitors. For example, there is a 15in-gauge line at Longleat and 10¼in-gauge lines at Audley End Estate, and Stapleford Park near Melton Mowbray, home of Lord Gretton.

All the new lines, and some of the older lines, now use a mixture of steam and diesel or petrol locomotives since, like full-size railways, miniature railway operators are finding that steam locomotives are not only becoming more costly but take time to get into steam. Staff is also a problem, as it is very difficult to obtain qualified drivers who are able to drive and maintain a complex piece of machinery like a steam locomotive. Moreover, at times of unexpected peak traffic, a diesel- or petrol-driven locomotive is usually available for instant service merely by pressing the starter button, whereas a steam locomotive can take anything up to 1½ hours to prepare from the time the fire is lit until it has sufficient head of steam to work a train.

During the late 1960s, a new company, Ian Allan Miniature Railway Supplies Ltd was formed for the supply, installation and operation of miniature railways, mostly of 10¼ gauge. This company in many ways resembles the old Bassett-Lowke-inspired Miniature Railways Ltd of almost 70 years ago in its activities, but brought up to date by specialising in diesel traction. In less than four years, the Ian Allan company has supplied equipment and, in most cases, jointly operates miniature railways at ten sites around the country, mostly seaside resorts including Bognor Regis, Hastings, Skegness and Prestatyn. Most of the lines are operated by a standard basic class of diesel locomotive known as the Meteor which embodies a Petter diesel engine with clutch and gearbox drive to the unusual 1-B-1 wheel arrangement. So far, nine Meteor locomotives have been built — probably rivalling Bassett-Lowke's *Little Giant* for the most numerous class of commercial miniature railway locomotive.

The line operated by the company at Hastings has been in existence for over 25 years and includes a mixture of steam and diesel traction. Another railway connected with the company is the 7¼in Great Cockrow Railway at Chertsey which has been rebuilt from the former Greywood Central Railway at Walton-on-Thames. This is a most ambitious line for it is fully signalled from three boxes with scale-size signals, and signalbox instruments of the same pattern as those used by British Railways to ensure the safe working of full-size trains. This emphasises that even on a miniature railway, as soon as more than one train is in operation, some form of signalling or operating sequence must be instituted to avoid collisions, for when carrying real live passengers, safety is of the utmost importance. On a complex line like the Great Cockrow Railway, where up to five or six trains may be in action at the same time, all loaded with passengers, clearly drivers and signalmen must be experienced operators fully conversant with the basic safety rules of full-size railways.

Whatever the type of miniature railway, whether for private use on an estate or for the public at a seaside resort or pleasure garden, they will always provide excitement for passengers young and old, regardless of whether steam or diesel traction is employed.

Top: Loading from a side ramp of two-deck car-carrier wagon of German Federal Railway. *DB Film Archiv*

Above: Between-decks view on a British Railways Cartic high-speed car carrier. *British Transport Films*

Bottom left: A British Rail train-load of Rootes cars/components in containers from the Chrysler Linwood (Scotland) factory at Annan in November 1971. *D Cross*

THE MODERN RAILWAY

Cars by Rail

FROM THE EARLY days of railways in Britain many carriage folk sent their equipages by train, usually the one in which they themselves were travelling, so as to be able to drive to and from the destination station. Not only did people travel *with* their carriages by rail, they even travelled *in* them, the vehicles being loaded on flat wagons. In the very early railway era, to ride in one's barouche-landau on the train was not only novel and daring but smart — exposed though one might be to whatever was coming out of the engine chimney. The practice was soon terminated by the railways, before it had time to catch on abroad on railways built after the pioneer lines of Britain.

As railways grew there was less tendency among carriage owners to take their vehicles by rail, for the road journeys at each end became shorter and people made increasing use of expanding public transport services. But there was always a steady carriage traffic, with passengers in railway coaches, on railways throughout the world during the horse age. The French Riviera winter season and the Scottish Highlands' later summer season both merited many express trains which included flat wagons to convey carriages for accompanying passengers to those resorts.

The old Highland Railway was indulgent to its deer-stalking and grouse-shooting customers (who were a large part of its bread and butter) and long allowed for carriage traffic in its best expresses; there is more than one vivid description of such a variegated caravan on the Perth-Inverness line. Continental railways tended to be stricter, largely because the attachment of flats carrying road vehicles would have overloaded trains that were already made up to the capacities of the locomotives available.

The advent of bogie carriages that could run at speeds higher than were deemed safe for four-wheel flats, and the economic need for maximum loads, kept carriage traffic off the fastest trains. Even so, up to the first world war there was one semi-fast train on the Great Northern Railway of Ireland between Dublin and Belfast that consisted largely of carriages (and a sprinkling of early motorcars) on flat wagons. During the 1930s it was possible also to take by Euston-Oban trains one or two motorcars in closed 'motorcar vans' that could run at speed; the trains would be stopped at wayside stations on the Callander to Oban line while the train engine placed the van at, or picked it up from, a loading dock.

Armies were the railways' biggest customers for movement of road vehicles in developed countries during the horse and early motor ages. Wars, summer manoeuvres and training camps all demanded special trains of vehicles and horses — and construction of the necessary loading docks. End-loading and side-loading can be seen at or near many stations and depots in Britain, and even more in Western Europe; most are today used by a new generation of car-carrier trains.

Deliveries of farm vehicles required some docks in rural areas but many such structures on the Continent were stategic. Most were completed before or during the 1914-18 war, when armies were still horse-transport minded. It is remarkable that so many proved strong enough for the heavy lorries — and later, tanks — that were developed so quickly in 1914-18. By 1939 there

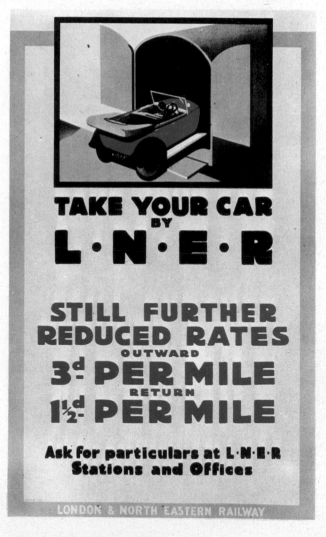

London and North Eastern Railway poster advertising its car-carrying service in 1931.
British Transport Museum (B Sharpe)

were loading docks capable of dealing with heavy lorries and bulky motor ambulances, some even with the lighter tanks and other tracked vehicles. Where docks did not exist, civilian railwaymen (and railway troops) were trained to improvise loading ramps with sleepers and other materials, and most station staffs were skilled in quick loading and unloading of wheeled and tracked road vehicles, and in prompt shunting of the flats and coupling them to or detaching them from trains.

Thus before the development of the private motorcar there existed the means and techniques for its movement by rail. One problem which caused little difficulty until the advent of the big lorry was loading gauge. Horse-drawn vehicles on flat wagons on broad- and standard-gauge railways were very seldom out of gauge. Even metre-gauge wagons could accommodate vehicles as much as 8ft in height and a little over 8ft broad, and there was no difficulty about length. Only the mass movement of road vehicles in double-deck wagons has necessitated special loading ramps at railheads.

Motorcars began to proliferate in the western world at the turn of the century. People who expected to see frequent brokendown cars on railway wagons were disappointed. Cars soon proved mechanically efficient — an i the very early pioneers usually managed to get a tow by a horse to a place where they could be repaired. There was little conveyance of cars by train to holiday resorts because motoring was quickly found to be pleasant along traffic-free and reasonably surfaced (except for *pavé*) main roads, while the commercial interests concerned soon organised convenient stations for the sale of petrol. This state of affairs continued until 1939 — by which time, however, there was already congestion on some roads in Britain and on the Continent at peak periods. But there were still not enough cars that needed to be moved on any one route to justify whole trains of cars; many long-distance trains did not convey flat wagons and most motorists disliked being parted from their vehicles.

Despite the increasing mechanical efficiency of the motorcar between the world wars, mountain roads could make for difficult motoring, partly because of the gradients and hairpin bends and partly because snow often lies on passes until well into the summer. Railways whose lines ran beneath mountain barriers in the Alps in tunnels were quick to cater for motorists who had no wish to brave difficult passes. A later development has been the demand for similar rail facilities for lorry haulage. The Swiss Federal Railways (SBB) many years ago started car-carrier trains through the Simplon and Gotthard tunnels; the Berne-Loetscheberg Simplon Railway (BLS) operates services for road vehicles through the Loetscheberg Tunnel; car-carrier trains of the metre-gauge Rhaetian Railway (RhB) traverse the Albula Tunnel; the Austrian Federal Railways (OBB) provides road vehicle services through the Arlberg and Tauern Tunnels; the Italian State Railways (FS) runs similar trains through the Mont Cenis Tunnel.

Except for the Albula service, which is limited to private cars and minibuses on account of the restricted loading gauge of the RhB, these trains convey private cars, motorcoaches and all but the largest lorries. Their terminals may be the stations adjoining the tunnel portals, or more distant stations, to allow the road vehicles to avoid long sections of difficult road or, especially in the case of road haulage vehicles, to

Right: German Federal car-carrying van for loading/unloading directly to/from station platform *E S Russell*.

Below: A German Federal new-car delivery train on the move from Wol Wolfsburg with both decks loaded. *DB Film Archiv*

Above: French National Railways double-deck car-carrier wagons in an Autorail train loading British tourists' cars at Channel port. *British Railways SR*

Right: Another view of a British Railways Motorail train being made ready for departure. *British Transport Films*

facilitate getting on and off the rail wagons at better-equipped stations. Recently the OBB has developed movement of bulky and heavy commercial road vehicles on low-loader wagons through the Arlberg tunnel between terminals some distance apart, since the mountainous part of the Arlberg Pass road begins and ends many miles away from each end of the tunnel.

The tunnel services are the result partly of the growth of road traffic — first passenger (largely tourist) and later freight — through the Alps and partly of railway electrification. In some cases drivers remain in their vehicles during the journey; but in any case passage of the tunnels was unpleasant in steam days. Services vary in frequency largely according to the season. The SBB trains through the Gotthard tunnel between Goeschenen and Airolo, both near the portals, run at 30-minute intervals even during the winter and take only 15 minutes to complete the transit. Loading and unloading are prompt sometimes by side and sometimes by end docks, or platforms, and on most services no prior notice is required for private cars and only short notice for commercial vehicles.

A river barrier can also be crossed by means of a tunnel. For many years until the opening of the Severn bridge the Great Western Railway and its successor the Western Region of British Railways ran car-carrier trains through the Severn Tunnel between Pilning in Gloucestershire and Severn Tunnel Junction in Monmouth. There have been many cases of conveyance of road vehicles on rail wagons for short distances over bridges or by train ferries; they are getting fewer as new road bridges are built and more special ferry vessels equipped for road vehicle transport are placed in service.

The manufacture and distribution of road vehicles from manufacturing plants involve operation of vehicle trains in all countries where traffic is on a big enough scale. North American railways, which do not carry accompanied cars on any appreciable scale, enjoy a large traffic of new cars and car parts and equipment; so in recent years do British and other railways in Western Europe. A problem in dealing with new cars is that of adjusting the order in which cars emerge from the manufacturing plant to that in which rail wagons are marshalled in a siding ready for dispatch to differing destinations, or of adjusting the marshalling of the wagons to that required by the order sheets. Where a whole train is concerned loading is of course much easier. Not all car plants have private sidings and cars might have to be driven to a railway depot.

Much of the traffic is moved on double-deck wagons so constructed as to allow vehicles to be driven along the upper deck from wagon to wagon when loading. Three-tier (tri-level) wagons are used in the USA and Canada, where the loading gauge allows greater height. Notable double-deckers are British Rail's high-speed Cartic quads, first introduced in 1964 and subsequently used in the Motorail trains conveying accompanied cars. The Cartic quad consists of four wagons each 46ft long and able to carry six average-size cars, three on each deck. The end wagons in each quad are carried on two-axle bogies at the outer ends but all other axles in the formation are singles, with floors sunk between the axles to provide maximum height between the decks. The big and dispersed British motorcar industry keeps busy a network of car trains over much of Great Britain between works and distribution centres and the sidings at ports for export traffic, with the car imports forming back loads.

Motorail is a term well known in Britain. The conveyance of accompanied motorcars on trains that include passenger accommodation — ordinary coaches for day and sleeping cars for night travel — with restaurant or buffet cars, originated in Britain, at least on a large scale. An incentive was the congestion on main roads that makes long-distance motoring so tiresome, which was first felt acutely in Britain, with its dense population and many cars. The first complete train in regular service carrying cars with their drivers and passengers was British Rail's Kings Cross to Perth 'carsleeper' of 1955; the passenger accommodation consisted, as the name implies, of sleeping cars. It was duly publicised and soon gained popular favour. What so pleased its patrons was the saving of the 450-mile drive — and of a probable night at a hotel en route — and the easy unloading at Perth and drive away into the Highlands, with a possibility of fetching up at most destinations that day without having to hurry.

Other services followed quickly, including some daytime services. All were planned to avoid many hours' motoring under the most unpleasant weekend or holiday season road conditions. The collective term Motorail was adopted in 1966. The creation of a new Motorail service is bound, even after careful market research, to be in some measure experimental; and public tastes tend to change. That is why some services have not lasted for more than a few seasons. But the remaining network operates on about 30 routes in Britain, some the year round and others seasonally.

The basic pattern is: night and/or day services between London, or a strategically located railhead serving a populous area in the provinces, on the one hand and a railhead serving a holiday area, or a Channel port, on the other. The railheads are chosen with an eye to the road approaches and the most likely sources of traffic in the surrounding areas. Departure and arrival times are determined partly with a view to the road journey before or after the train trip. The chief Motorail terminal in London is at Kensington Olympia, which was specially built and includes all necessary modern amenities. Motorail trains comprise car-carrier wagons (including Cartics) and sleeping and ordinary passenger coaches. After early arrival of overnight trains passengers may remain undisturbed in their sleepers until about 7.30 in the morning, when breakfast is available at the station. The day trains include restaurant cars.

A feature of British Motorail is the absence of tiresome restrictions in booking, though obviously one must book in reasonable time for journeys during the high season. In most cases cars need not be presented for loading more than an hour before departure time. Documentation is rationalised and simple. All these factors have added to the popularity of Motorail and several Continental railways have followed suit, setting up a substantial and growing Autorail network, using car-carrier wagons resembling those of British Rail but built to the rather bigger European loading gauge.

The greater distances on the European mainland mean a greater proportion of car-sleeper trains, as opposed to day trains, than in Britain. Many night trains are not merely overnight but involve some hours of daytime travel as well. The Hook of Holland to Ljubljana (Jugoslavia) car-sleeper, which runs in con-

nection with the Harwich-Hook day steamer, takes about 19 hours overall, and the Hook to Poznan (Poland) car-sleeper 16 hours. Not all night trains incorporate sleeping cars in the proper sense of that word; the accommodation on some services is simply *couchettes* — berths with pillows and rugs, quite comfortable but not affording the luxury of sleeping cars. Some trains run from ports, for example, the Hook, Ostend, Boulogne and Dieppe, in connection with sailings from and to England, and Britons form a large proportion of car-sleeper customers. Nearly all trains run to and from a tourist centre or well-chosen railhead, such as Biasca in the Swiss canton of Ticino, on the main road to Italy as it drops down from the Gotthard Pass.

Biasca is the terminus for car-sleepers from the Hook of Holland and you can leave London one morning, put your car on the day boat to the Hook and be on Lake Como in good time for lunch next day — or in Venice by dinner time.

The only Continental daytime car-carrier trains are in Italy and Federal Germany, but car-sleeper trains run in Spain, France and Belgium, through Luxembourg, and in Holland, Federal Germany, Austria, Switzerland and Italy. Their routes criss-cross Western Europe. As car ownership grows and the discomfort and danger of long-distance motoring increase, Continental Motorail services tend to multiply — but not fast. Their growth is checked largely by the high cost of the car-carrier wagons, which are also needed by the expanding motorcar manufacturing industry.

Car distribution from factories by rail, and goods vehicle 'piggyback' services are both on a large-scale in North America, but until recently Motorail had not caught on, probably because motoring over long distances is pleasanter than in the more built-up conditions of Europe. Another powerful reason is that Canadians and Americans in recent years have not been railway minded; railways for passenger travel have dropped out of many people's consciousness, and railway managements, which for many years lost money on their long-distance passenger business, have hesitated to invest money in new passenger commitments.

Now however comes news of the new Autotrain service that has been carrying winter holidaymakers and their cars between the North-East and Florida. From a railhead in the suburbs of Washington it runs overnight over the Richmond Fredericksburg & Potomac and Seaboard Coastline Railroads to Sanford in Florida, nearly 1,000 miles. It is organised and the wagons are supplied by a separate organisation and the railways simply provide the diesel locomotives, track and signalling. The wagons are covered double-deckers with room for drivers and passengers, who ride in their own vehicles, to walk past the cars to the coaches that include buffet and washrooms.

Top right: Car delivery direct from factory floor to dealer by standard 40ft container. The Auto Perch lightweight cradle supports car rear to pack in maximum number. *Apex Photos Ltd*

Bottom right: BR Motorail train of Cartics and regular passenger coaches, *British Transport Films*

Below: French CC6500 8,000hp high-speed locomotive heads the Trans Europe Express Le Rhodanien in 1971. *'La Vie du Rail'*

Inset right: Ae8/14 11,100hp 68mph electric locomotive for heavy freight working. *Swiss Federal Railways*

Inset lower: New German Class 420 suburban electric multiple-unit train has all axles motored and high installed power for good acceleration in stopping service. *Db Film Archiv*

Facing page: Impressive front end of German Class 103 electric locomotive, one of which has been developed to provide a short-term output of 14,000hp. *DB Film Archiv*

Power Unlimited

A GLANCE AT the smooth and often elegant exterior of an electric locomotive gives little clue to the variety of equipment inside. Here, within the limits set by the railway loading gauge, the designer has to accommodate a complex assembly of switchgear, rotary machines and heavy static items, planning the layout to distribute the weight evenly over the locomotive underframe and carrying driving bogies.

Different types of electrical installation are necessary for alternating current (ac) and direct current (dc) locomotives, although some features are common to both. Among common equipment are the motor-driven blowers which continuously supply cooling air to the traction motors. The cooling requirement — perhaps 3,500 cubic feet of air per minute to each motor, is a reminder of the virtually unlimited power in the supply network on which an electric locomotive can draw.

Electric traction motors are given two horse-power ratings — for continuous and one-hour performance.

Both are based on temperature rise, because the electric motor converts electrical into mechanical energy and no conversion process is 100 per cent efficient. Some of the energy appears as heat, which must be carried away by the stream of cooling air or else the temperature of the motors would rise to a level which would damage them.

Motors can be allowed to work harder for one hour than continuously, and so the one-hour rating can be up to about 20 per cent higher than the continuous. Over very short periods the output can be higher still sometimes approaching double the continuous. This advantage is unique to the electric locomotive. It is not shared by any other form of motive power — steam, diesel, or gas turbine, all of which are limited to the capacity of the primary power plant carried on board.

The heating of the motors is related to current flowing, and this is shown on meters in the driving cab. Often part of the meter scale is coloured red to warn the driver that the pointer must only be allowed to stay there for a short time. Much has been done in recent years to improve the materials used in traction motor construction, particularly in their insulation, so that high temperatures can be tolerated for longer, and maximum use can be made of reserve power from the network for rapid acceleration after speed reductions and recovering lost time.

In early electric locomotives the body between the end cabs was virtually an engine room, the traction motors being mounted on the main frames and occupying much of the interior. The drive was transmitted from the motor shafts to the axles by various rod systems corresponding to the connecting and coupling rods of a steam locomotive. The geometry of the driving systems allowed for relative movement between the motors and the axles due to the springs, but the high motor mountings and heavy rods tended to make the locomotives top-heavy and unstable at speed. Therefore the next step was to transmit the drive through gears, as had electric motor coaches. In locomotives, however, much larger motors were involved, because all the power required to haul a train had to be concentrated in one motive power unit instead of being distributed through the train. The motor coach practice of using small axle-hung motors in the bogies was not practicable and motors continued to be mounted on the main frames of the locomotives.

Designers still had the problem of accommodating changes in the centre-to-centre distance of the drives as the suspension springs flexed. Gearwheels could not be mounted directly on the axles because they would not mesh accurately with the motor pinions. Generally the solution was to mount the gearwheel on a hollow shaft, or quill, running in bearings at a fixed distance from the motor shaft, and to pass the axle through the quill with sufficient clearance for it to move up and down while revolving. The drive from quill to axle was provided by one of many forms of flexible linkage.

As long as traction motors remained on the main frames, the driving wheelbase had to be fixed, as in a steam locomotive, and so electric locomotive wheel arrangements followed steam locomotive patterns, with non-motored carrying axles in bogie or pony trucks fore and aft. Main-line locomotives were being built to this pattern right up to the 1950s. It was seen in the 4,000hp 4-8-4 locomotives built for the Paris to Lyons electrification of the French National Railways opened in 1952. These were descendant of a long line of French locomotives of the same wheel arrangement, and by the time they went into service another form of electric locomotive construction had already emerged, and one which was soon to become universal.

This new concept for main-line electric traction can be dated from four 4,000hp locomotives built for the Berne-Lotschberg Railway in Switzerland in 1945. Here for the first time it had been found possible to accommodate motors of 1,000hp in the bogies, taking advantage of advances in electrical and mechanical design and materials. The improvements were not confined to the motors, but extended to the design of the bogies themselves and the suspension of the body on them, so that the bogies could fill the dual function of driving and guiding the locomotive. Every axle was now a driving axle, and the whole weight of the locomotive was used for adhesion. The pattern for the modern electric locomotive had been set.

In electric locomotive wheel arrangement notation, motored axles are denoted by a letter (B for 2, C for 3 and so on) and non-motored axles by a figure. When an axle is driven by its own motor, a small letter 'o' is written after the letter. The Berne-Lotschberg-Simplon locomotives had two two-axle bogies, every axle driven by its own motor, and so their designation is Bo-Bo. In the French National Railways 4,000hp locomotives mentioned earlier there is a two-axle bogie at front and rear and a fixed four-axle driving wheelbase with independently-driven axles. This is the same as a steam 4-8-4 (steam notation being based on numbers of wheels, not axles). In electric notation it becomes 2-Do-2.

British main-line electrification began in the 1930s on the Southern Railway, and at first services were operated entirely by motor-coach trains under multiple-unit control, freight continuing to be steam-hauled. At the beginning of the second world war, however, two 1,470hp electric locomotives were introduced on the SR for freight work and passenger services which could not be formed of multiple-unit stock, such as through trains to other parts of the railway system, and boat trains. These locomotives had two three-axle bogies with individual drive (Co-Čo). After the war numbers of 1,868hp four-axle (Bo-Bo) and 2,700hp six-axle (Co-Co) locomotives were built for freight and passenger work on the Eastern Region electrification between Sheffield and Manchester.

In all these designs the motors were of under 500hp and were axle-hung in the bogies in the same way as in motor coaches. In axle-hung suspension about half the motor weight rests directly on the axle, the remainder being supported from the bogie frame by some form of resilient mounting which allows the motor to rise and fall with movements of the axle. The more powerful motors in Continental locomotives of the same period, however, were solidly attached to the bogie frames so that the whole of their weight was spring-borne. As in the case of the earlier practice of carrying motors on the main frames, quill drives with flexible linkages were required, but by that time such transmissions were becoming lighter and smaller, and required less maintenance.

With the London Midland Region 25kV ac electrification from Euston to Manchester and Liverpool in the 1960s the need for more-powerful electric locomotives arose in Britain, and the first designs were Bo-Bos of about 3,300hp, so that individual motor outputs were around 850hp. All the first 100 new locomotives followed the Continental practice of fully spring-borne motors in the bogies with flexible drives to the axles. Flexible transmissions had long been a source of controversy among traction engineers, and one school of thought held that the modern traction motor could stand up to the shocks it received at speed when axle-hung. The second series of 100 locomotives for the Euston-Manchester-Liverpool routes, rated at first at 3,600hp, but later increased in some cases to 4,000hp, reverted to axle-hung motors. However, since their introduction in 1967 experience has shown that the use of fully spring-borne motors is justified on high-speed

Top: Netherlands Railways Class 1100 80-ton Bo-Bo of about 3,000hp. *B Bond*

Inset right: Control desk of a BR Class 86 4,000hp Bo-Bo electric. *D N Jamieson*

Inset lower: Swiss type Re4/4 Bo-Bo electric.of 6,320hp for Trans Europe Express service. *Swiss Federal Railways*

Below: German type 184 electric locomotive for international working directly from any one of four types of power supply, two ac and two dc. *DB Film Archiv*

routes by the saving in wear and tear of the permanent way. This practice will be followed in new 5,100hp locomotives for the electrification extension to Glasgow.

For most of the 1960s the favoured type of main-line electric locomotive was a Bo-Bo of about 80 tons weight and a rating between 3,000 and 5,000hp. This was true for all systems of electrification. After dropping the 2-Do-2 type in favour of a Co-Co wheel arrangement in the early 1950s, the French National Railways started experimenting with Bo-Bo designs and soon ordered them in large numbers both for its 1,500V dc and 25kV ac lines. South Africa had imported from Britain in the 1950s some 3,030hp 3,000V dc electric locomotives with two three-axle motor bogies and carrying axles fore and aft (1Co-Co1), but its next order was for a Bo-Bo of 2,020hp, the policy being to double-head trains when more power was needed. In the latest version of the Bo-Bo locomotives the output has been raised to 3,340hp by improvements in motor design. These are remarkable achievements considering the dimensional constraints of the 3ft 6in gauge of South African Railways.

The same trend was seen on railways with low-frequency ac electrification. Switzerland followed its 6,000hp Co-Cos for the Gotthard line with a prototype 5,540hp Bo-Bo equipped for working in pairs when necessary, and later uprated a production series to 6,050hp. After a locomotive standardisation programme in Western Germany the railways were equipped with several Bo-Bo classes, the most powerful of which was rated at 4,850hp.

It is a sign of the vigour of the railway industry that nothing is static. Already the Co-Co locomotive is beginning to reappear for certain duties which were barely contemplated a decade ago. The need to maintain tractive effort at speeds up to 125mph has brought the demand for still higher horsepower and so the 8,000hp electric locomotive carried on two three-axle bogies is now a reality. Germany has its 103 class for low-frequency ac, and France its 21000, 14500 and 6500 classes, the first covering both standard-frequency ac (50Hz) and 1,500V dc operation, and the other two being for standard-frequency ac and 1,500V dc respectively.

It is still general practice for each axle of an electric locomotive to be driven by its own motor, but there are some noteworthy exceptions. In several French locomotive classes there is only one large motor in each bogie and this drives all axles through trains of gears. Often two ratios are provided and can be selected from inside the locomotive when it is at a standstill. In this way the range of duties that can be undertaken economically by one locomotive — already wide in electric traction — is still further extended. The coupling of the axles in each bogie through the gears reduces the chance of wheelspin on greasy rail.

The biggest changes in the internal equipment of electric locomotives have taken place on railways using 25kV ac at the standard industrial frequency of 50Hz. As on any ac system, the largest single piece of apparatus is the transformer, with which there is usually associated a motor-driven tap-changer to control the voltage applied to the traction motors. Between the transformer and the motors, however, it is now usual to connect semiconductor rectifiers which convert the ac into dc. There is always a residula 'ripple' in dc produced by rectifying a single-phase supply such as is used on railways and this is minimised by smoothing chokes, which in themselves are quite bulky and heavy items to fit into a locomotive.

A dc supply is also needed to charge the locomotive battery, because certain essential services must be battery-powered if there is no supply for traction. Usually this auxiliary dc is taken from a separate small rectifier instead of from a motor-generator set.

In some ac locomotives the traction rectifiers consist partly of thyristors, which both rectify the ac input and allow the dc output voltage to be controlled electronically without using a tap-changer. It is not practicable for one group of thyristors to cover the whole range from zero to the full traction motor voltage and so the cells are arranged in two or more groups which act in sequence. Some switching may be involved in changing from group to group, but it is much simpler than the conventional tap-changing process and varies the voltage so gradually that the system is often called 'stepless control'. Sudden increases in voltage as the driver increases power when starting a heavy train can start wheelspin, and so the smooth build-up possible with thyristors enables the best use to be made of the adhesive weight of the locomotive.

In dc traction the motor voltage is still usually controlled by resistances and changes of motor grouping. Exceptions are the Southern Region electric and electro-diesel (electric with auxiliary diesel power) locomotives in which power from the third rail drives a motor-generator set. The generator output first opposes and then boosts the third-rail supply, which process enables the voltage applied from zero to maximum without wasting power in resistances in the main motor circuit.

Another alternative to resistance control for dc locomotives is just coming into the picture. It is called 'chopper' control, and uses thyristors as on/off switches which act in a similar way to the contacts of a vibrating voltage regulator. Installations are working satisfactorily in motor coaches, and a 3,000V dc chopper locomotive is ready for trials in Italy.

Getting an electric locomotive on the move with its train by increasing the power — 'notching up' — calls for skill in keeping the current within the safe limits. In most modern locomotives the driver's controller has two main positions. In one position the equipment notches up automatically, but the process can be stopped at any stage by moving the lever back a step. The second position enables the driver to notch up manually by moving the lever up to it and back again. Each to-and-fro action advances the equipment one notch.

In addition to the development of locomotives for the separate ac and dc systems, recent years have seen the emergence of locomotives able to work on both types of supply. The ac locomotive with rectifiers has made this possible, because it is 'half dc' anyway, and so when it reaches dc territory the supply is simply switched directly to the power circuit, bypassing the transformer and rectifiers. Belgium, France and Germany all have locomotives which can work on the two ac systems (low- and standard-frequency) and the two dc voltages (1,500V and 3,000V) used on the main lines of the European Continent. Some countries remain faithful to the systems of electrification they have developed over many years, but the traveller in the international electric expresses of today passes from one system to another without being aware of it.

Ground Transport of the Future

TRAINS ABOUT TO enter experimental service in several countries seem likely to take maximum speeds to around 150mph and point-to-point averages of substantially over 100mph will probably become common within a few years on many of the world's major railway routes.

There might well be development of wheeled trains to speeds beyond those presently envisaged; many railwaymen believe there will be, perhaps using the linear induction motor to bypass anticipated problems of loss of wheel adhesion in driving and braking at high speed. Others think that, as the next step upward in speed will require new and probably different forms of track that will require high capital expenditure anyway, the time is ripe to exploit one of the newer types of high-speed ground transport that might have considerably more development potential than the conventional railway. So, we have enlisted the help of an expert in the field to take a look at the possibilities of the popularly so-called hovertrain system under development in several countries.

Broadly speaking the problems associated with achieving high vehicle speeds without contact with the ground resolve themselves into three main areas, namely, (1) levitation, (2) guidance, and (3) propulsion. It will be noted that the problem of vehicle control is common to all high-speed systems whether they are levitated or wheeled. Many of the requisite techniques are already hard experimental fact, so much so that it is now possible to travel at 185mph in comfort and safety in the French 80-seat prototype *Orleans* hovercoach. Speeds up to 265mph have been reached in smaller experimental craft.

At first inspection the solutions to levitation and guidance might appear to be necessarily the same, but this need not be the case. At the other extreme, as was demonstrated in model form at the recent American Transpo 72 exhibition in Washington, a single electro-magnetic technique is available which will satisfy all three requirements in one self-contained system.

There are three practical techniques available which are capable of producing the forces necessary to achieve levitation and guidance:

1. Pressurised ambient air — Air cushions.
2. Electromagnetic attraction — Ferro-magnetism.
3. Induced eddy-current repulsion — Superconducting magnets.

Unlike air cushions, electromagnetic techniques in their simplest form are liable to be statically unstable. Static stability can only be achieved if one degree of freedom is retrained, for example, by wheels, or if time-varying magnetic fields are employed. In the case of electromagnetic attraction, the natural stiffness of the system (that is, the increase in attractive force as the magnetic surfaces move closer together) has to be reversed. It can be done by using an external closed-loop controller which acts to reduce the magnet excitation current, and therefore attractive force, as the running clearance between magnet and rail is reduced. The presence of a time-varying magnetic field is inherent in the induced eddy-current process since the very process itself depends on the forward movement of the vehicle. Permanent magnets are not on their own an acceptable solution since their magnetic field is constant. A vehicle levitated by permanent magnets would require additional lateral restraint.

Two techniques are available for achieving contactless propulsion, namely, (1) aerodynamic reaction by propellers or turbojets, and (2) electromagnetic reaction by linear induction motors. In order to be acceptable to public opinion, it is generally recognised that future propulsion systems must be pollution free and as quiet as possible. In addition, operational requirements demand that the propulsion unit must be capable of operating in limited enclosures, for example, tunnels, and be generally easy to control and automate. While early attempts to produce a practicable prototype

The Krauss-Maffei magnetically levitated vehicle which has on board dc magnets acting against U-shaped rails attached to a concrete track. *Krauss-Maffei*

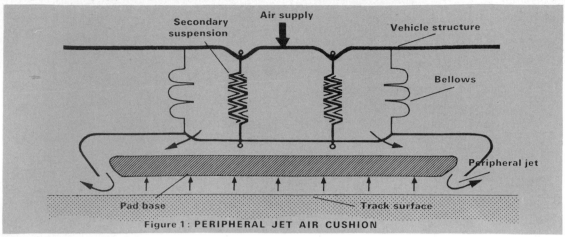

Figure 1: PERIPHERAL JET AIR CUSHION

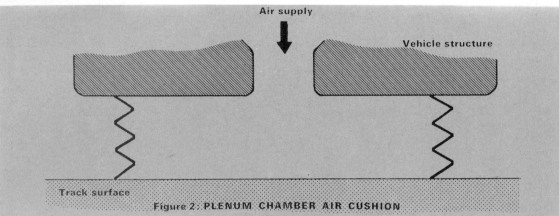

Figure 2: PLENUM CHAMBER AIR CUSHION

hovercoach have adopted ducted propellers as the means of propulsion (the French *Orleans* vehicle) the general tendency must be towards electromagnetic propulsion. All the systems described below are powered by linear induction motor (LIM).

A LIM propulsive unit consists of two parts, the primary wound part called the stator, which is carried on the vehicle, and the secondary part called the reaction rail, which extends along the full length of the track. When the stator is supplied with three-phase alternating current a travelling magnetic field is created which in turn produces a useful thrust force between the stator and reaction rail.

Air cushions which can be used for lift and guidance have sprung from a simple experiment with a pair of cocoa tins and a hair-drying blower, which established the hovering principle. In the mid-nineteen-fifties Sir Christopher Cockerell showed that if pressurised air was ducted down the annual space between two tins of slightly different diameter placed just above a supporting surface, then the load-carrying capability over that provided by a single tin was markedly improved. Thus was born the idea of the peripheral-jet air cushion. Since that time a great deal of development has taken place, particularly in this country, to improve upon the performance of the basic concept. The principle of operation is shown in Fig 1. Inward-facing jets round the periphery of the pad set up a momentum barrier which traps pressurised air beneath the central base of the pad, which acts to produce useful lift. Typical air-cushion pressures are of the order of 2 to 3lb per square inch above ambient.

The French have put a great deal of effort into the development of the simpler plenum chamber type of air cushion, shown in Fig 2. In order to optimise their efficiency, pads of this type depend on the adoption of smaller running clearances (0.1 to 0.2in) between the sidewalls and the track surface. This in turn demands the use of flexible skirts. Generally speaking, the pads are of relatively low pressure of about 0.5lb/sq in (further to reduce the air leakage rate) and consequently have to be of larger area than a peripheral jet to support a given vehicle weight.

The French have adopted an inverted T-section track for all their hovertrain vehicles. The vehicles are guided by additional air cushions which act on the sides of the vertical stem. The prototype 44-seat *Suburbain* vehicle illustrated is typical of the general arrangement adopted.

Test equipment installed in one of the trailer cars of the APT set.

Above: First shown in
the summer of 1972, the
APT-E evolved by
British Rail

Left: The French Suburbain
hovertrain prototype is
driven by a linear motor.
Bertin & Cie

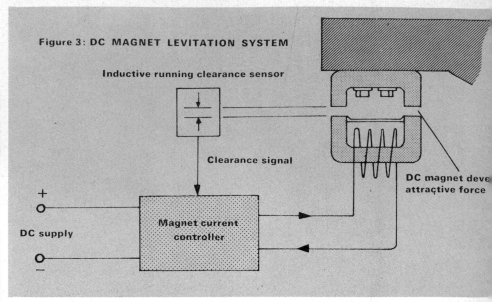

Figure 3: DC MAGNET LEVITATION SYSTEM

Inductive running clearance sensor

Clearance signal

DC supply

Magnet current controller

DC magnet deve
attractive force

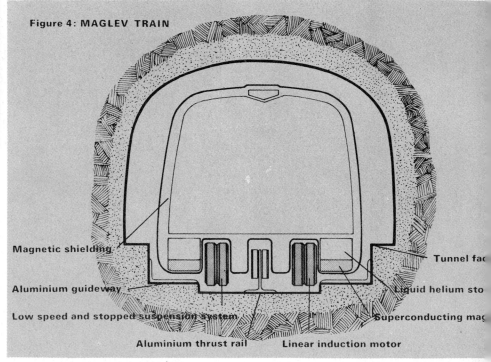

Figure 4: MAGLEV TRAIN

Magnetic shielding

Aluminium guideway

Low speed and stopped suspension system

Aluminium thrust rail

Linear induction motor

Tunnel fac

Liquid helium sto

Superconducting mag

Left top to bottom: The MBB research
vehicle which is lifted by the magnetic
attractive force developed between the
magnet and its associated ferromagnetic
rail. *Messerschmitt-Bolkow-Blohm*

The driver's cabin of the MBB vehicle
showing the simplicity of the controls.
Messerschmitt-Bolkow-Blohm

In this view the magnets attached to
the vehicle may be seen positioned under
the rail. *Messerschmitt-Bolkow-Blohm*

The British Tracked Hovercraft is seen
here on its experimental track in
Cambridgeshire. *Tracked Hovercraft Ltd*

In this instance the vehicle is driven by a linear motor so the central stem of the track is made of aluminium in order that it can also act as the reaction rail for the motor.

Both the British and some American work have opted for the peripheral jet pad in tracked air cushion research vehicle programmes. Pads of this type can operate satisfactorily at larger running clearances (0.5 to 0.75), with consequent reduction in the incidence of possibly harmful contact between pad and track. Typically, a peripheral jet pad will consume half the power of the equivalent plenum pad at the same running clearance. The secondary suspensions in the British research vehicle are housed inside the large ·diameter bellows which supply air to the hover-pads (see Fig 1).

The Americans have chosen a channel-section track, while the British company, Tracked Hovercraft Ltd, has selected a rectangular-section track in which the vehicle is guided by air cushions which bear on the vertical sides of the box beams. Both research vehicles are propelled by linear induction motor, the Americans using a double-sided motor with the free upstanding reaction rail placed centrally in the base of the trough. The British have adopted a single-sided configuration in which the reaction rail lies flush in the top surface of the track.

Of more recent origin than air cushions, a significant research and development programme has been launched in West Germany to investigate the use of ferro-magnetic attraction for lift and guidance of high-speed trains. Two passenger-carrying research vehicles are now running. The basic method of operation of the direct-current (dc) excited magnet is shown in Fig 3. The vehicle is lifted by the magnetic attractive force which is developed between the magnet and its associated ferromagnetic rail. Note that the magnets are attached to the vehicle and are positioned underneath the rails which extend along the full length of the track.

The running clearance between the magnet and rail is measured by an inductive height sensor. The sensor produces a continuous signal which is proportional to the running clearance and this is fed back to the magnet controller. The controller in turn varies the magnet excitation current and therefore the attractive force developed between the magnet and the rail. As the attractive force is increased the running clearance will reduce the vice versa. The closed-loop control system thus acts in such a way that the running clearance between magnet and rail is held nearly constant to a predetermined value and stable levitation is thereby achieved.

A similar technique can be used to achieve contactless guidance. The track consists of two substantial steel angles which are supported on appropriate brackets. The vehicle is supported by a first set of magnets which act underneath the horizontal surface of the rails and is guided by a second set of magnets which act against the vertical faces of the rails. The vehicle is propelled by a doubled-sided linear induction motor. Two magnetically levitated vehicles are illustrated; the MBB is as described above and the one by Krauss-Maffei has on-board dc magnets which act against U-shaped rails attached to a concrete track.

The use of eddy-current repulsion for lift and guidance represents the most futuristic system proposed for high-speed trains. It involves the use of super-conducting magnets with their associated cryogenic cooking equipment carried on board each vehicle.

When a magnet moves with a certain velocity across a conducting sheet, the magnetic flux emanating from the magnet will couple with the sheet and produce circulating currents in it. The circulating currents will generate their own field which will tend to oppose the action of the original field and thus the magnet will be repelled by the sheet. The magnitude of the repulsive force will depend on the speed of the magnet relative to the sheet but more particularly on the intensity of the magnetic field produced by the magnet.

The discovery of superconductivity has enabled very high-intensity magnetic fields to be produced for a negligible consumption of electric power. A substance is said to be a superconductor when its electrical resistance is effectively zero. Certain alloys, niobium-zirconium for example, exhibit this property when they are cooled to very low temperatures (below minus 269 degrees Centrigrade). The resistance less state enables very large currents to flow through the material without any power losses and if the material is shaped in the form of a closed loop then once started the currents will flow round the loop perpetually. If, therefore, the coils of a magnet are held in the superconducting state an intense magnetic field can be produced without the expenditure of any power regardless of the field intensity or dimensions of the coil.

Early theoretical and model work on eddy-current repulsion techniques has been carried out mainly in the United States. The Sandia Laboratories in New Mexico have investigated the possibility of supporting a high-speed rocket-propelled test sled on superconducting magnets and accelerating the payload up to 11,000mph in an evacuated tube to reduce aerodynamics drag.

The work on the rocket sled project has led to a proposal for a high-speed passenger train running on a conducting sheet guideway. The general arrangement of the Maglev train, as it is called, is shown in Fig 4. The superconducting magnets and associated cooling equipment are housed in the side sponsons of the vehicle. The vehicle runs within two L-shaped aluminium rails. The horizontal parts directly under the magnets provide lift and lateral stability is provide lift and lateral stability is provided by the vertical members. Typically, six superconducting magnets each carrying a current of 300,000 amperes will levitate a 100-passenger vehicle weighing 50,000lb to a real clearance of three inches above the aluminium rails. The operating speed in open atmosphere would be of the order of 300mph.

Since the repulsive levitating forces are only generated at forward speed it is necessary to have pneumatic-tyred wheels to support the vehicle at low speeds. The vehicle will lift off at about 50mph. The circulating currents which are generated in the sheet guideway (which is not superconducting) represent a power loss which is experienced as a drag force acting on the vehicle. The additional magnetic drag has to be overcome by the linear motor propulsive system. Magnetic drag is a fundamental feature of all systems using eddy-current repulsion as the means of levitation. Its minimisation is one of the main areas of interest occupying the minds of the promotors.

So there we have it, not one but three practical techniques for achieving a levitated vehicle system. The final choice will depend upon economics, environmental considerations and operational requirements. different applications might dictate different optimum solutions.

Turbo Trains At Last

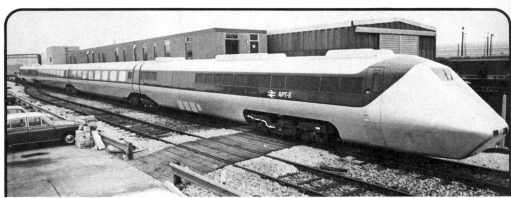

Top: French National Railways ETG turbotrain on the regular Paris-Caen-Cherbourg service. *SNCF*

Top centre: First British Railways gas turbine-powered mu, the experimental advanced passenger train about to start track testing in July 1972. *British Railways*

Left: One of the French ETG turbotrains at Caen station in July 1970. *J Winkley*

Below: French experimental gas turbo-electric advanced passenger train's first appearance at Belfort in April 1972. *La Vie du Rail (Y Broncard)*